In The Dust
of This Planet

[Horror of Philosophy, vol. 1]

In The Dust
of This Planet

[Horror of Philosophy, vol. 1]

Eugene Thacker

Winchester, UK
Washington, USA

JOHN HUNT PUBLISHING

First published by Zero Books, 2011
Zero Books is an imprint of John Hunt Publishing Ltd., No. 3 East St., Alresford,
Hampshire SO24 9EE, UK
office@jhpbooks.com
www.johnhuntpublishing.com
www.zero-books.net

For distributor details and how to order please visit the 'Ordering' section on our website.

ISBN: 978 1 84694 676 9
978 1 78099 010 1 (ebook)

A CIP catalogue record for this book is available from the British Library.

Design: Stuart Davies

UK: Printed and bound by CPI Group (UK) Ltd, Croydon, CR0 4YY
US: Printed and bound by Thomson-Shore, 7300 West Joy Road, Dexter, MI 48130

CONTENTS

Also in the series:

Clouds of Unknowing

The life of every individual, viewed as a whole and in general, and when only its most significant features are emphasized, is really a tragedy; but gone through in detail it has the character of a comedy.
~ Arthur Schopenhauer

...when you are "nowhere" physically, you are "everywhere" spiritually...Never mind if you cannot fathom this nothing, for I love it surely so much the better.
~ The Cloud of Unknowing

The world is increasingly unthinkable – a world of planetary disasters, emerging pandemics, tectonic shifts, strange weather, oil-drenched seascapes, and the furtive, always-looming threat of extinction. In spite of our daily concerns, wants, and desires, it is increasingly difficult to comprehend the world in which we live and of which we are a part. To confront this idea is to confront an absolute limit to our ability to adequately understand the world at all – an idea that has been a central motif of the horror genre for some time.

The aim of this book is to explore the relationship between philosophy and horror, through this motif of the "unthinkable world." More specifically, we will explore the relation between philosophy as it overlaps with a number of adjacent fields (demonology, occultism, and mysticism), and the genre of supernatural horror, as it is manifest in fiction, film, comics, music, and other media. However, this relationship between philosophy and horror should not be taken to mean "the philosophy of horror," in which horror as a literary or film genre is presented as a rigorous formal system. If anything, it means the reverse, *the horror of philosophy*: the isolation of those moments in which philosophy reveals its own limitations and constraints, moments in which thinking enigmatically confronts the horizon of its own possibility – the thought of the unthinkable that philosophy cannot pronounce but via a non-philosophical language. The genre of supernatural horror is a privileged site in which this paradoxical thought of the unthinkable takes place. What an earlier era would have described through the language of darkness mysticism or negative theology, our contemporary era thinks of in terms of supernatural horror.

In this book, the means by which philosophy and horror are related to each other is the idea of the "world." But the world can mean many things, from a subjective experience of living in the world, to the objective, scientific study of geological conditions. The world is human and non-human, anthropocentric and non-anthropomorphic, sometimes even misanthropic. Arguably, one of the greatest challenges that philosophy faces today lies in comprehending the world in which we live as both a human *and* a non-human world – and of comprehending this politically.

On the one hand, we are increasingly more and more aware of the world in which we live as a non-human world, a world outside, one that is manifest is the effects of global climate change, natural disasters, the energy crisis, and the progressive extinction of species world-wide. On the other hand, all these effects are linked, directly and indirectly, to our living in and living as a part of this non-human world. Hence contradiction is built into this challenge – we cannot help but to think of the world as a human world, by virtue of the fact that it is we human beings that think it.

However, this dilemma is not necessarily new. Philosophy has repeatedly returned to this problem of the non-human world. While in philosophy circles today it may be called "corre-lationism," "accelerationism," or "atmospheric politics," for earlier philosophers this same dilemma was expressed in different terminology: the problem of "being-in-the-world," the dichotomy between "active" or "passive" nihilism, or the limits of human thought in the "antinomies of reason."

When the world as such cataclysmically manifests itself in the form of a disaster, how do we interpret or give meaning to the world? There are precedents in Western culture for this kind of thinking. In classical Greece the interpretation is primarily *mythological* – Greek tragedy, for instance, not only deals with the questions of fate and destiny, but in so doing it also evokes a world at once familiar and unfamiliar, a world within our control or a world as a plaything of the gods. By contrast, the response of Medieval and early modern Christianity is primarily *theological* – the long tradition of apocalyptic liter-ature, as well as the Scholastic commentaries on the nature of evil, cast the non-human world within a moral framework of salvation. In modernity, in the intersection of scientific hegemony, industrial capitalism, and what Nietzsche famously prophesied as the death of God, the non-human world gains a different value. In modernity, the response is primarily *existential* – a questioning of the role of human individuals and human groups in light of modern science, high technology, industrial and post-industrial capitalism, and world wars.

The contemporary cynic – which on many days describes myself – might respond that we still live by all of these inter-pretive frameworks, and that only their outer shell has changed – the mythological has become the stuff of the culture indus-tries, spinning out big-budget, computer-generated films and merchandise; the theological has diffused into political ideology and the fanaticism of religious conflict; and the existential has been re-purposed into self-help and the therapeutics of consumerism. While there may be some truth in this, what is more important is how all of these interpretive lenses – mytho-logical, theological, existential – have as their most basic presup-position a view of the world as a human-centric world, as a world "for us" as human beings, living in human cultures, governed by human values. While classical Greece does, of course, acknowledge that the world is not totally within human control, it nevertheless tends to personify the non-human world in its pantheon of humanoid creatures and its all-too-human gods, themselves ruled by jealously, greed, and lust. The same can be said of the Christian framework, which, while also personifying the supernatural (angels and demons; a paternal God by turns loving and abusive), re-casts the order of the world within a moral-economic framework of sin, debt, and redemption in a life after life. And the modern existential framework, with its ethical imperative of choice, freedom, and will, in the face of both scientific and religious determinisms, ultimately constricts the entire world into a solipsistic, angst-ridden vortex of the individual human subject. In short, when the non-human world manifests itself to us in these ambivalent ways, more often than not our response is to recuperate that non-human world into whatever the dominant, human-centric worldview is at the time. After all, being human, how else would we make sense of the world?

However, one of the greatest lessons of the ongoing discussion on global climate change is that these approaches are no longer adequate. We can, instead, offer a new terminology for thinking about this problem of the non-human world. Let us call the world in which we live the *world-for-us*. This is the world that we, as human beings, interpret and give meaning to, the world that we relate to or feel alienated from, the world that we are at once a part of and that is also separate from the human. But this world-for-us is not, of course, totally within the ambit of human wants and desires; the world often "bites back," resists, or ignores our attempts to mold it into the world-for-us. Let us call this the *world-in-itself*. This is the world in some inaccessible, already-given state, which we then turn into the world-for-us. The world-in-itself is a paradoxical concept; the moment we think it and attempt to act on it, it ceases to be the world-in-itself and becomes the world-for-us. A significant part of this paradoxical world-in-itself is grounded by scientific inquiry – both the production of scientific knowledge of the world and the technical means of acting on and intervening in the world.

Even though there is something out there that is not the world-for-us, and even though we can name it the world-in-itself, this latter constitutes a horizon for thought, always receding just beyond the bounds of intelligibility. Tragically, we are most reminded of the world-in-itself when the world-in-itself is manifest in the form of natural disasters. The discussions on the long-term impact of climate change also evoke this reminder of the world-in-itself, as the specter of extinction furtively looms over such discussions. Using advanced predictive models, we have even imagined what would happen to the world if we as human beings were to become extinct. So, while we can never experience the world-in-itself, we seem to be almost fatalistically drawn to it, perhaps as a limit that defines who we are as human beings.

Let us call this spectral and speculative world the *world-without-us*. In a sense, the world-without-us allows us to think the world-in-itself, without getting caught up in a vicious circle of logical paradox. The world-in-itself may co-exist with the world-for-us – indeed the human being is defined by its impressive capacity for not recognizing this distinction. By contrast, the world-without-us cannot co-exist with the human world-for-us; the world-without-us is the subtraction of the human from the world. To say that the world-without-us is antagonistic to the human is to attempt to put things in human terms, in the terms of the world-for-us. To say that the world-without-us is neutral with respect to the human, is to attempt to put things in the terms of the world-in-itself. The world-without-us lies somewhere in between, in a nebulous zone that is at once impersonal and horrific. The world-without-us is as much a cultural concept as it is a scientific one, and, as this book attempts to show, it is in the genres of supernatural horror and science fiction that we most frequently find attempts to think about, and to confront the difficult thought of, the world-without-us.

In a sense, the real challenge today is not finding a new or improved version of the world-for-us, and it is not relentlessly pursuing the phantom objectivity of the world-in-itself. The real challenge lies in confronting this enigmatic concept of the world-without-us, and understanding why this world-without-us continues to persist in the shadows of the world-for-us and the world-in-itself. We can even abbreviate these three concepts further: the world-for-us is simply the *World*, the world-in-itself is simply the *Earth*, and the world-without-us is simply the *Planet*. The terms "world" and "worlding" are frequently used in phenomenology to describe the way in which we as human subjects exist in the world, at the same time as the world is revealed to us. By contrast, we understand the "Earth" as encompassing all the knowledge of the world as an object, via geology, archaeology, paleontology, the life sciences, the atmospheric sciences (meteorology, climatology), and so on.

What then is the "Planet"? The World (the world-for-us) not only implies a human-centric mode of being, but it also points to the fuzzy domain of the not-human, or that which is not for-us. We may understand this in a general sense as that which we cannot control or predict, or we may understand it in more concrete terms as the ozone, carbon footprints, and so on. Thus the World implicitly opens onto the Earth. But even "the Earth" is simply a designation that we've given to something that has revealed itself or made itself available to the gathering of samples, the generating of data, the production of models, and the disputes over policy. By necessity there are other character-istics that are not accounted for, that are not measured, and that remain hidden and occulted. Anything that reveals itself does not reveal itself in total. This remainder, perhaps, is the "Planet." In a literal sense the Planet moves beyond the subjective World, but it also recedes behind the objective Earth. The Planet is a planet, it is one planet among other planets, moving the scale of things out from the terrestrial into the cosmological framework. Whether the Planet is yet another subjective, idealist construct or whether it can have objectivity and be accounted for as such, is an irresolvable dilemma. What is important in the concept of the Planet is that it remains a negative concept, simply that which remains "after" the human. The Planet can thus be described as impersonal and anonymous.

In the context of philosophy, the central question today is whether thought is always determined within the framework of the human point of view. What other alternatives lay open to us? One approach is to cease searching for some imaginary locus of the non-human "out there" in the world, and to refuse the well-worn dichotomy between self and world, subject and object. This is, of course, much easier said than done. In addition to the interpretive frameworks of the mythological (classical-Greek), the theological (Medieval-Christian), and the existential (modern-European), would it be possible to shift our framework to something we can only call *cosmological*? Could such a cosmo-logical view be understood not simply as the view from inter-stellar space, but as the view of the world-without-us, the Planetary view?

Scientists estimate that approximately ninety percent of the cells in the human body belong to non-human organisms (bacteria, fungi, and a whole bestiary of other organisms). Why shouldn't this also be the case for human thought as well? In a sense, this book is an exploration of this idea – *that thought is not human*. In a sense, the world-without-us is not to be found in a

7

"great beyond" that is exterior to the World (the world-for-us) or the Earth (the world-in-itself); rather, it is in the very fissures, lapses, or lacunae in the World and the Earth. The Planet (the world-without-us) is, in the words of darkness mysticism, the "dark intelligible abyss" that is paradoxically manifest as the World and the Earth.

Hence, a central focus of this book is on the problem of thinking this world-without-us; and its argument is that this problem is at once a philosophical, a political, and a cultural problem. Hence the subtitle of the series, of which this book is a part: "horror of philosophy." But here a terminological clarification is in order. The term "horror" does not exclusively mean cultural productions of horror (or "art horror"), be it in fiction, film, comics, or video games. While the horror genre is an important part of culture, and while scholarly studies of the horror genre do help us to understand how a book or film obtains the effects it does, genre horror deserves to be considered as more than the sum of its formal properties. Also, by "horror" I do not mean the human emotion of fear, be it manifest in a fiction film, a news report, or a personal experience. Certainly this type of horror is an important part of the human condition, and it can be leveraged in different ways – ethically, politically, religiously – for the gain of different ends. This also deserves to be studied, especially for the ways in which reality and fiction increasingly overlap in our reality-TV culture. But "horror" in this sense remains strongly inscribed within the scope of human interests and the world-for-us.

Against these two common assumptions, I would propose that horror be understood not as dealing with human fear in a human world (the world-for-us), but that horror be understood as being about the limits of the human as it confronts a world that is not just a World, and not just the Earth, but also a Planet (the world-without-us). This also means that horror is not simply about fear, but instead about the enigmatic thought of the unknown. As H.P. Lovecraft famously noted, "the oldest and strongest emotion of mankind is fear, and the oldest and strongest kind of fear is the fear of the unknown." Horror is about the paradoxical thought of the unthinkable. In so far as it deals with this limit of thought, encapsulated in the phrase of the world-without-us, horror is "philosophical." But in so far as it evokes the world-without-us as a limit, it is a "negative philosophy" (akin to negative theology, but in the absence of God).

Briefly, the argument of this book is that *"horror" is a non-philosophical attempt to think about the world-without-us philosophically.* Here culture is the terrain on which we find attempts to confront an impersonal and indifferent world-without-us, an irresolvable gulf between the world-for-us and the world-in-itself, with a void called the Planet that is poised between the World and the Earth. It is for this reason that this book treats genre horror as a mode of philosophy (or, perhaps, as "non-philosophy"[1]). Certainly a short story about an amorphous, quasi-sentient, mass of crude oil taking over the planet will not contain the type of logical rigor that one finds in the philosophy of Aristotle or Kant. But in a different way, what genre horror does do is it takes aim at the presuppositions of philosophical inquiry – that the world is always the world-for-us – and makes of those blind spots its central concern, expressing them not in abstract concepts but in a whole bestiary of impossible life forms – mists, ooze, blobs, slime, clouds, and muck. Or, as Plato once put it, "hair, mud, and dirt."

I. Three *Quæstio* on Demonology

Between the 11th and 13th centuries, much of Western philosophy was developed within the then-emerging universities, many of which were institutionally tied to the Church, though not without a great deal of controversy. During this period of "scholastic" thinking, a number of discursive forms were introduced that have become the basis for modern philosophy and its tenuous connection to the modern university. The *lectio*, for instance, is the forerunner of our modern "lecture," while the *disputatio* is the forerunner of our modern classroom debate or discussion. Originating in the medieval law schools, the *quæstio* or "question" developed as a systematic way to compare canonical legal texts, as well as the commentaries attached to them. When discrepancies were found in the same law developed in a different region or at a different time, this became the occasion for an inquiry or "questioning," the goal of which would be to achieve some sort of synthesis or reconciliation of the discrepancies.

By the 12th century, philosophers and theologians incorporated the *quæstio* into their own teaching as a way of systematically exploring a topic – usually one associated with or deriving from theological matters. This, combined with the resurgence in the study of Aristotle's logical works, led to the kind of methodical, almost detective-like investigation of a concept that one finds in, for instance, the works of Thomas Aquinas. But the use of the *quæstio* did not have strict rules. Aquinas sometimes incorporates *quæstio* within the larger framework of the *summa* (the "summary" or compendium), while at other times the *quæstio* are themselves the framework (as in his work *De Malo*, or "On Evil").

What follows here are three *quæstio* which deal broadly with demonology, understood as the study of demons and the demonic. Historically speaking, demons are far from being horned and goateed Mephistos tempting us to do bad things. The demon is as much a philosophical concept as it is a religious and political one. In fact, the "demon" is often a placeholder for some sort of non-human, malefic agency that acts against the human (that is, against the world-for-us).

Borrowing from thinkers such as Aquinas, each *quæstio* utilizes the simple format of the statement of a theme, a discussion of assumptions on that theme (*articulus*), and a discussion of counter-arguments (*sed contra*), before attempting to find some middle way or resolution (*responsio*) – which, needless to say, often ends up in irresolution and more questions.

QUÆSTIO I – On the Meaning of the Word "Black" in Black Metal

ARTICULUS

Demons abound in popular culture, and yet we longer believe in demons – at least, this is the story we tell ourselves. If we do indeed live in enlightened, technological times, we also live in a "post-secular" era in which the themes of religion, theology, and mysticism seep back into our world, often in obtuse ways. A case in point is black metal. Black metal is not just a music genre, but also a subculture and a way of thinking about demons and the demonic in a world of religious extremes. While black metal bands rarely put forth anything like a systematic philosophy of horror, the music, lyrics, and iconography of black metal are relevant for the ways in which they look back to earlier concepts of demons and the demonic – in all their ambiguity. In a way, there is no better starting point for the "horror of philosophy" than black metal.

Certainly, discussions of music genres often revolve around what does or doesn't constitute the essence of that genre. When disagreements arise, a common solution is simply to divide the genre into subgenres. Metal is no exception to this pattern, and there are more and more metal subgenres every day. Metal is no longer just heavy, but also death, speed, grind, doom, funeral, and of course black. That said, while there is no shortage of discussion on metal as a music genre, there is less discussion on all the adjectives that make one subgenre distinct from another, adjectives that belie a set of concepts and orientations. What, for example, is the "black" in black metal? In its popular associations, black metal is called black for a wide range of reasons – its references to black magic, demons, witchcraft, lycanthropy, necromancy, the nature of evil, and all things somber and funereal. Black metal is black because it is – this is one argument at least – the most extreme form of metal, both in its attitude and in its musical form.

Of all these associations, there is one thing that sticks out, and that is the association of black metal to Satanism and the figure of the Devil. In fact, it would seem that this equation is the defining factor of black metal: *Black = Satanism*. Obviously this is a reduction, and we will undo it later on. To begin with, however, we have to keep in mind the complicated history of translation and terminology, as the term *satan* or *ha-satan* passes from the Hebrew Bible (where it designates an angelic divinity that tests one's faith) to the Koine Greek of the Septuagint, to the Latin Vulgate of the Old Testament, before its appearance in the Gospels, where the figure of Satan is often depicted as a malefic figure poised against the monotheistic God, rather than against humanity per se. At different points in the long history of Christianity, the figure of the Devil, as the universal antagonist of God and humanity, is given different names, Satan being only one of them, and it is with this figure with which the "black" in black metal may arguably be identified. Certainly black metal is neither the only metal subgenre, nor the only music genre generally, to have made this association. One can just as easily find it in the music of Robert Johnson or the *Carmina Burana* as one could in bands like Black Sabbath. But the degree to which Satanism constitutes a conceptual reference point for black metal is indeed striking.

For the moment, then, let us think about "black" as meaning Satanic. What does this imply conceptually? For one, if we take the Medieval and early Renaissance notion of Satan as a starting point, the equation black = Satanism is governed by a structure of opposition and inversion. Opposition defines the demonic as much as the divine; it is the "War in Heaven" described so vividly in *Revelations*, and dramatized in Milton's *Paradise Lost*. Opposition is also the structure that comes to define the Medieval Church against its foes, the role that the Church councils accord various activities, from witchcraft to necromancy, as threats to both religious law and religious political authority. This opposition, then, is as much political as it is theological, resulting in the infamous witch-hunts, persecutions, and inquisitions of the early Renaissance. In its oppositional mode, the equation black = Satanic means "against God," "against the Sovereign," or even "against the divine."

The image of Satanism takes on a different form by the 19th century, however. In a sense, one cannot really talk about Satanism before this time, at least not as an organized counter-religion complete with its own rituals, texts, and symbols. What we would call Satanism before this time was, legally speaking, defined by the Church as heresy, and heresy is a particular kind of threat – it is not the threat of not believing at all, but the threat of believing in the "wrong" way. By contrast, 19th century Europe, following upon the religious challenges posed by Romanticism, the Revolution, and the aesthetics of the gothic and decadent movements, developed something that more resembles modern Satanism. It is markedly different from the Medieval and early Renaissance versions as it is from its later-20th century incarnations (e.g. Anton LaVey's Church of

Satan). This more formalized, "poetic" Satanism operated not only by opposition, but also by inversion, as demonstrated in Charles Baudelaire's then-scandalous poem "Les Litanies de Satan" (1857). This Satanism is ritually, as well as ideologically, opposed to the Church. In its 19th century context, it overlaps considerably with occultism, magic, and even offshoots of spiritualism. A key aspect of this poetic Satanism is the infamous Black Mass, deliriously portrayed in Joris-Karl Huysmans' novel *Là-bas* (1891; *Down There*) – which is purportedly based on a real Black Mass the author had attended. Every element of the Black Mass, from the blasphemous anti-prayer to the erotic desecration of the host, aims at an exact inversion of the Catholic High Mass.

If we take the "black" in black metal to mean Satanic, then we see how this is emblematic of a conceptual structure of opposition (its Medieval, "heretical" variant) and inversion (its 19th century, "poetic" variant). In this association we also see a relation to the natural world and supernatural forces as the means through which opposition and inversion is effected. The "black" in this case is almost like a technology, or a dark technics. Black magic in particular is predicated on the ability of the sorcerer to utilize dark forces against light, one set of beliefs against another.

SED CONTRA

On the contrary, it is obvious to any listener of black metal that not all black metal bands ascribe to this equation of black = Satanic. There are many black metal bands that take a non-Christian framework as their foundation, referencing everything from Norse mythology to the mysteries of ancient Egypt. We can take a different approach, then, and suggest another meaning to the word "black" in black metal, and that is: *Black = pagan*. We will undo this yet again, but for the time being let us think about this in contrast to the black = Satanism meaning.

To begin with, paganism denotes less a negative or reactive mode, than an entirely different, and ultimately pre-Christian outlook. Historically, the different forms of paganism overlap with the rise of Christianity as a dominant religious, juridical, and political force. Paganism, as a polytheistic – and sometimes pantheistic – viewpoint, stood in stark contrast to the doctrinal sovereignty of the Church. Because of this, forms of paganism were often inculcated within what the Church ambiguously called heresy. During the high Renaissance a wide range of activities, from alchemy to shamanism, were popularly associated with paganism. The ideas of Rosicrucianism, Freemasonry, Hermeticism, and, in the 19th century, theosophy and spiritualism, all claimed some connection to a pagan outlook. The ambit and scope of some of these movements is even more expansive than Christianity itself; the writings of Madame Blavatsky and Rudolph Steiner, for instance, are exemplary in their trans-cultural and trans-historical breadth. In books such as *Isis Unveiled* (1877) or *The Secret Doctrine* (1888), Blavatsky covers everything from archaic mystery cults to modern paranormal research, giving one the sort of global perspective found in anthropology classics such as James Frazer's *The Golden Bough* (1890).

While these different forms of paganism sometimes overlap with the traditional Judeo-Christian outlook, more often than not they are marginalized, and, in some cases, driven underground into secret societies. Here we see one major difference from the prior association of "black" with Satanism. Whereas the latter operated through opposition and inversion, the former is related to the dominant framework of Christianity by exclusion and alterity. Whereas heresy was viewed by the Church primarily as an internal threat, with paganism one finds, in some cases, an entirely different framework – an external threat. The iconography is also different. Instead of demonic invocations and the Black Mass, there may be images of animistic nature, elemental and earth powers, astral lights and astral bodies, the metamorphoses of human and animal, human and plant, and human and nature itself. In paganism one is always "on the side of" nature and its animistic forces. The magician is less one who uses nature as a tool, and more like a conduit for natural forces. Whereas in Satanism one finds an attempt to instrumentalize dark forces against light, in paganism magic is technology and vice-versa. Works like Eliphas Lévi's *Dogme et Rituel de la Haute Magie* (1855) read like a veritable how-to book of occult knowledge, theories, and practices. In contrast to the dark technics of Satanism, then, the dark magic of paganism.

RESPONSIO

So far, we have two possible meanings that the word "black" can have in black metal culture. These are black = Satanism and black = paganism. One has the structure of opposition and inversion, and other the structure of exclusion and alterity. Both are united, however, in what amounts to a human-oriented relation to nature and natural forces – with Satanism we see a dark technics of dark vs. light forces, and with paganism we see a dark magic of being-on-the-side of nature itself. Despite their differences, both meanings of the term "black" point to one thing they have in common, and that is an anthropocentric view towards the world. The world is either there for us to use as a tool, or it is there inside us as a force for our benefit. Even as the various forms of paganism adopt an animistic or pantheistic view of the world, they also assert a means of knowing and utilizing the forces of that world; the self is at once united with the world and yet split from it. The human point of view seems to be a limit for thought in both of these meanings of "black" (Satanism and paganism).

Is there yet another meaning of "black" beyond this? There is, but it is a difficult thought to think, and nearly impossible to know, though it does exist (actually it doesn't exist, though the thought of its not-existing does). As we noted, both the Satanic and pagan variants of the word "black" remain minimally committed to the perspective of the human, even as they posit forces in the world beyond all comprehension. The result is that these dark forces are in some way always "for us" as human beings (either as wielding darkness or "being on the side of" darkness). Whereas both the Satanic and pagan variants retain an anthropocentric thread, a third position, which we can call "cosmic," attempts to relinquish even this. There is only the anonymous, impersonal "in itself" of the world, indifferent to us as human beings, despite all we do to change, to shape, to improve and even to save the world. We could be even more specific and refer to this perspective not just as cosmic, but as a form of "Cosmic Pessimism." The view of Cosmic Pessimism is a strange mysticism of the world-without-us, a hermeticism of the abyss, a noumenal occultism. It is the difficult thought of the world as absolutely unhuman, and indifferent to the hopes, desires, and struggles of human individuals and groups. Its limit-thought is the idea of absolute nothingness, unconsciously represented in the many popular media images of nuclear war, natural disasters, global pandemics, and the cataclysmic effects of climate change. Certainly these are the images, or the specters, of Cosmic Pessimism, and different from the scientific, economic, and political realities and underlie them; but they are images deeply embedded in our psyche nonetheless. Beyond these specters there is the impossible thought of extinction, with not even a single human being to think the absence of all human beings, with no thought to think the negation of all thought. Hence another possible meaning of the term "black": Black = Cosmic. Or better, *Black = Cosmic Pessimism.*

Cosmic Pessimism has a genealogy that is more philosophical than theological. Its greatest – and most curmudgeonly – proponent was Arthur Schopenhauer, the misanthrope who rallied as much against philosophy itself as he did against doctrinal religion and the nationalist politics of his time. Throughout his life, Schopenhauer remained equally dissatisfied with the meticulous system building of Kant as with the nature-Romanticism of Fichte, Schelling, and Hegel. If we are to really think about the world as it exists in itself, Schopenhauer says, we have to challenge the most basic premises of philosophy. These include the principle of sufficient reason (everything that exists has a reason for existing), as well as the well-worn dichotomy between self and world, so central to modern empirical science. We have to entertain the possibility that there is no reason for something existing; or that the split between subject and object is only our name for something equally accidental we call knowledge; or, an even more difficult thought, that while there may be some order to the self and the cosmos, to the microcosm and macrocosm, it is an order that is absolutely indifferent to our existence, and of which we can have only a negative awareness.

The most we can do, Schopenhauer notes, is to think this persistence of the negative. He uses the term *Vorstellung* (Representation; Idea; Conception) to describe this negative awareness, an awareness of the world as we conceive it (be it through subjective experience or through aesthetic represen-tation), or the world as it is presented to us (be it through practical knowledge or scientific observation). Whatever the case, the world remains the world-for-us, the world as *Vorstellung*. Is there something outside this? Logically there must be, since every positive needs a negative. Schopenhauer calls this non-existent something-outside *Wille* (Will; Drive; Force), a term that designates less the volition or action of an individual person, and more an abstract principle that runs through all things, from the bowels of the earth to the array of constellations – but which is not in itself anything.

Unlike his Romantic contemporaries, however, Schopenhauer views this abstract *Wille* as impersonal, blind, and indifferent to our wants and desires. There is no nature-for-us, much less any being-on-the-side-of nature. Furthermore, the *Wille* is, in itself, "nothing," a gulf at the heart of the world as *Vorstellung*. The *Wille*, as an impersonal nothing, is also inseparable from a negation that paradoxically constitutes the world, but which ultimately negates even itself (becoming "Willlessness"). In contrast to what Schopenhauer calls a privative nothing (the *nihil privativum*; dark as the absence of light, death as the absence of life) there is a negative nothing (the *nihil negativum*; nothingness without any positive value). The opaque last words of *The World as Will and Representation* encapsulate this paradoxical affirmation of nothing:

> ...what remains after the complete abolition of the Will is, for all who are full of the Will, assuredly nothing (*Nichts*). But also conversely, to those in whom the Will has turned and denied itself, this very real world of ours with all its suns and galaxies, is – nothing.[2]

Schopenhauer is unparalleled in this sort of metaphysical misanthropy, this type of cosmic pessimism. Even a thinker such as Nietzsche, who otherwise lauds Schopenhauer as one of his "educators" and great anti-philosophers, chooses to recuperate Schopenhauer's pessimism into a more vigorous, vitalistic, "Will-to-Power." Schopenhauer's pessimism is less about a human pessimism (e.g. the all-too-human despair of an identity crisis or a lapse in faith), and more about the way in which thought in itself always devolves upon its own limits, the hinge through which positive knowledge turns into negative knowledge. To find an equal to Schopenhauer, one would have to look not to philosophy but to writers of supernatural horror such as H.P. Lovecraft, whose stories evoke a sense of what he termed "cosmic outsideness":

The most merciful thing in the world, I think, is the inability of the human mind to correlate all its contents. We live on a placid island of ignorance in the midst of black seas of infinity, and it was not meant that we should voyage far. The sciences, each straining in its own direction, have hitherto harmed us little; but some day the piecing together of dissociated knowledge will open up such terrifying vistas of reality, and of our frightful position therein, that we shall either go mad from the revelation or flee from the deadly light into the peace and safety of a new dark age.[3]

In summary, then, another meaning of the word "black" – not Satanism with its opposition/inversion and dark technics, not paganism with its exclusion/alterity and dark magic, but a Cosmic Pessimism, with its dark metaphysics of negation, nothingness, and the non-human.

What do these different conceptual aspects of "black" mean in relation to black metal culture? On the surface, it would seem that black metal bands would fall into one of these three meanings of the word "black." For instance, old school Norwegian black metal would seem to fit the Satanic meaning of black, as evidenced by albums such as Darkthrone's *Transylvanian Hunger*, Emperor's *Wrath of the Tyrant*, Gorgoroth's *Pentagram*, and Mayhem's *De Mysteriis Dom Sathanas*. Likewise, it would seem that other black metal bands might fit the pagan meaning of black, as exhibited by Ulver's *Nattens Madrigal*, Ildjarn's *Forest Poetry*, Striborg's *Mysterious Semblance*, and Wolves in the Throne Room's *Diadem of Twelve Stars*. One could even suggest that some of the formal experiments in black metal, from the minimalism of Sunn O)))'s *Grimmrobe Demos* to the wall-of-noise in Wold's *Stratification* might offer musical equivalents of the Cosmic Pessimism meaning of the word black.

I would suggest, however, that this third kind of "black," that of Cosmic Pessimism, is actually implicit in all of the above examples, though in differing degrees.

In this sense, the most striking example of Cosmic Pessimism comes from outside of the metal genre altogether. It is by the Japanese multi-instrumentalist, poet, and mystic Keiji Haino. Haino's album *So, Black is Myself* employs a subtractive minimalism that is beyond that of Sunn O))) or dark ambient artists such as Lustmord. Haino's approach is eclectic, borrowing techniques from everything from Noh theater to Troubadour singing. Clocking in at just under 70 minutes, *So, Black is Myself* uses only a tone generator and voice. Its sole lyric is the title of the piece itself: *"Wisdom that will bless I, who live in the spiral joy born at the utter end of a black prayer."* The piece is brooding, rumbling, deeply sonorous, and meditative. Sometimes the tone generator and Haino's voice merge into one, while at other times they diverge and become dissonant. Haino's voice itself spans the tonal spectrum, from nearly subharmonic chant to an uncanny falsetto perhaps produced only by starving banshees. Haino's performance is an example of the radically unhuman aspect of Cosmic Pessimism, the impersonal affect of dread described by Kierkegaard as "antipathic sympathy and sympathetic antipathy." *So, Black is Myself* also manages to be mystical at the same time that the individual performer is dissolved into a meshwork of tones – voice, space, and instrument variously existing in consonance and dissonance with each other. *So, Black is Myself* is a reminder of the metaphysical negation that is also at the core of black metal, as if Schopenhauer's *nihil negativum* were rendered as musical form, ultimately negating even itself in a kind of musical anti-form.

QUÆSTIO II – On Whether There are Demons, and How to Know Them

ARTICULUS

That demons really exist seems to be verified by the cross-cultural acceptance of supernatural forces of some type, that may be rendered to varying degrees as animalistic or anthropomorphic, and that display a general antagonism towards all of humanity (and in some cases, the world itself). Scholarship in comparative mythology and religion has done much to reveal the similarities and the differences between demons of this type. The *jinn* in Islamic theology and pre-Islamic mythology, the *se'irim* of the Hebrew Bible, and the legion of evil spirits in the Judeo-Christian tradition, all testify to some type of supernatural antagonism that may manifest itself within theistic ways of understanding the world. Other claims have also been made for demon or demon-like equivalents in various African, Polynesian, and Native American folklore traditions, as well as in the Hindu and Buddhist pantheons (in the *Tibetan Book of the Dead*, for instance, one encounters, as part of the Bardo cycle, the "dawning of wrathful deities").

However, it seems that our technologically advanced, scientifically hegemonic, and religiously conservative post-millennium world leaves little room for something as fanciful as demons. At the most, such flights of fancy are left to the culture industries, where demons swarm about (via advanced computer graphics) in films, television, and video games. Even within the culture industry, there is the subgenre of Satanic cinema – from "documentaries" such as *Häxan*, to Hollywood films like *The Exorcist*, to recent indie films like *House of the Devil*. In films like these, the elaborate scenes of exorcisms and possession serve to remind us that what we today classify as mental illness was, for an earlier era, a manifestation of the demonic.

Nevertheless, one must still account for the persistence of the figure of the demon, even as it is relegated to the fringes of genre fantasy and horror. One way of doing this is to understand the demon less in a strictly theological sense, in which the demon is the relation between the supernatural and natural, and to understand it in its cultural function as a way of thinking about the various relationships between human individuals and groups. In short, the figure of the demon, though it may not be accepted literally today, can be understood in an anthropological framework, as a metaphor for the nature of the human, and the relation of human to human (even when this relation is couched in terms of the boundary between human and non-human).

In fact, it is possible to outline an anthropology of the demon in Western culture with this perspective in mind. We could begin with the *daimōn* (δαιμων) in classical Greece, found in Hesiod and Homer as well as in the works of Plato. There the demon is not a malevolent or malefic figure, but a divine entity that may serve as a source of inspiration, that may also serve to warn or to caution. When Socrates claims to always have by his side a "demon" (*daimonion*) that prevents him from taking the wrong course of action, he is invoking this more elemental meaning of the demon. The Greek demon is, in a sense, very much in keeping with the classical themes of human free will and destiny vis-à-vis the will of the gods.

The association of the demon with malevolent and malefic forces is most commonly made in early Christianity, though, as we've noted, there are arguments for its development in early Judaic and Islamic theology as well. The archetypal example of this is the demon as tempter, as told in Athanasius' *Life of Antony*. While meditating in the desert, Anthony is repeatedly assaulted by demons, which take the form of everything from tempestuous winds to Satyrs and Centaurs. After closing himself off in a desert cave, Anthony is again assaulted by demons. "The demons, as if breaking through the building's four walls, and seeming to enter through them, were changed into the forms of beasts and reptiles."[4] Despite the pains he endures, Anthony's asceticism and prayer remains unfaltering, and the demonic assault is to no avail. This motif of immovable prayer against the temptations of the demon has also become something of an iconographic image of the demonic in Western art.

An interesting shift takes place once one moves into the clinical and medical view of Western modernity. In a 1923 article, "A Neurosis of Demonical Possession in the Seventeenth Century," Freud re-casts an account of possession in light of psychoanalysis's study of the workings of the unconscious. In terms of historical accounts of possession, the case study itself is unremarkable. It involves Christoph Haitzmann, a young painter who, in or around 1677, sees a priest, complaining of convulsions, hallucinations, and a sense of persecution. Aside from being an artist, the priest finds nothing wrong with Haitzmann – except, of course, that he may be in consort with a demon. Like the case study, Freud's analysis is also unremarkable. Tracing Haitzmann's delusions to the death of his father, Freud then remarks that the demon is a condensed "father-substitute" – at once a replacement for Haitzmann's mourned loss, as well as a crisis brought about by the absence of the father as a figure of authority. As per the standard psychoanalytic reading, the demon is taken to be an externalized projection, and the so-called possession really a form of therapeutic purging for Haitzmann himself.

We might even attempt a further permutation, in which the demon is neither purely theological nor psychological, but sociological. Here the political aspects of the demon, as the stand-in for a threatening Other, come to the fore. The demon becomes a name, a placeholder, a designation that signifies at once that which is outside and, because of this, that which is a threat. Exemplary in this regard is recent scholarship in comparative religious studies. Elaine Pagels's widely-read *The Origin of Satan* makes the clearest point: the demon is inseparable from a process of demonization, and this process is as much political as it is religious. Whether, as in Pagels's study, the demonic refers to pagans (the threat from outside), or to non-Christian Jews (the boundary between outside and inside), or, finally, to acts of heresy within Christianity (the threat from inside), all follow this motif of naming an Other.

If the demon is taken in this anthropological sense as the relation of the human to the non-human (however this non-human is understood), then we can see how the demon historically passes through various phases: there is the classical demon, which is elemental, and at once a help and a hindrance (*"the demon beside me..."*); there is the Medieval demon, a supernatural and intermediary being that is a tempter (*"demons surround me..."*); a modern demon, rendered both natural and scientific through psychoanalysis, and internalized within the machinations of the unconscious (*"I am a demon to myself..."*); and finally a contemporary demon, in which the social and political aspects of antagonism are variously attributed to the Other in relationships of enmity (*"demons are other people"*).

SED CONTRA

Let us return to the traditional, Christian-theological premise of the demon – demons are, generally speaking, both malevolent and malefic. They are understood as supernatural beings that intend to do evil to humanity, and do so through supernatural means. Whether they are rendered as monstrous, chimerical creatures, or as invisible and immaterial dark forces, the demon often inhabits the edges of the human understanding of the world. This twofold characteristic – an antagonism towards the human, and some form of supernatural mediation – are a key part of the theological concept of the demon. By the time one arrives at modern psychoanalysis, the antagonism is internalized (perhaps via some personal trauma) and the mediation is medicalized (for example, as a form of clinical paranoia). Even in such cases, however, the manifestation of the phenomena in question is taken as if the antagonism is external, and as if the mediation comes from the outside. This twofold character remains, if only in a more secular and more scientific framework. The "as if" is important, since for a previous era the "as if" was taken quite simply "as is."

In the interpretations of the demon above, the demon functions as a metaphor for the human – both in the sense of the human's ability to comprehend itself, as well as the relations between one human being and another. The demon is not really a supernatural creature, but an anthropological motif through which we human beings project, externalize, and represent the darker side of the human to ourselves. While this may serve a certain therapeutic function, something is lost in this anthropological interpretation of the demon, and that is the way in which the antagonism so central to the demon is also a non-human antagonism, an antagonism that is beyond human comprehension – not natural but supernatural, not merely physical but metaphysical. But how is the traditional Christian-theological demon non-human, when again and again in sacred texts demons are represented in decidedly anthropomorphic ways?

One way of understanding the non-human aspect of the demon is to understand the demon less in a strictly theological sense, in which the demon is an intermediary creature between the supernatural and natural, and to understand it in its ontological function as a way of thinking about the relation of the human to that which is non-human. This vague, latter term – the non-human – can, of course, have a wide range of meanings, from the rock or the chair to the black depths of the cosmos itself. And we as human beings certainly have a panoply of ways of relating to the non-human, be it via science, technology, politics, or religion. But the non-human remains, by definition, a

26

limit; it designates both that which we stand in relation to and that which remains forever inaccessible to us. This limit is the unknown, and the unknown, as genre horror reminds us, is often a source of fear or dread.

Thus, in contrast to the anthropological interpretation of the demon, we can consider another one that is *mythological*. By this term we imply more than the human understanding of the human, and instead move outwards to the human understanding of the world. The mythological interpretation of the demon takes place less by the use of metaphor, and more by the use of allegory, in which the very story of our ability or inability to comprehend the world is encapsulated in the ritual acts of invasion, possession, metamorphosis, and exorcism.

This comes through more clearly in one of the classic Biblical accounts of demonic possession, that of the so-called Gerasene demon. Slightly different accounts are given in *Mark* 5 and *Luke* 8, but the basics of the parable are the same: Jesus, with his followers, travels from Galilee to the Gerasene region (in northern current-day Jordan). There Jesus is met by the local villagers, who appeal to him to heal an old man possessed by demons. The possessed man, it is said, roams about the tombs without clothing or shelter. When the villagers shackle him, he enters into a frenzy and breaks free. At night he screams aloud and cuts himself with stones. Jesus confronts the possessed man, who likewise appeals to Jesus to cure him. As part of the exorcism, Jesus commands the name of the demon possessing the old man: "Then Jesus asked him, 'What is your name?' 'My name is Legion,' he replied, 'for we are many.'"[5] The name "Legion" (λεγων) is tricky, for it is not clear from the passage whether it is a single demon speaking in many voices, or if it is a multitude of demons speaking in a single voice. Indeed, the very name "Legion" appears to devolve upon itself, the name of the Many naming itself as One. Jesus then casts the demons out of the body of the old man, and into a herd of swine in a nearby hill. The herd of swine, now possessed, are driven into a state of frenzy and rush over the side of a cliff into the sea below to their death. After this rather dramatic episode, something interesting happens: the villagers, witnessing the entire spectacle, become fearful of Jesus and his healing powers. With some urgency they politely ask Jesus and his followers to leave the village.

In this parable the demons manifest themselves in three ways, each an example of the limits of the human to comprehend the non-human. First, within the possessed man are a multitude of demons. Demonic possession itself transgresses the normal relationship between the One and the Many (one person = one body). It is also an affront to and parody of the Trinity, in which a single One is incarnated in Three. God as Creator creates many creatures. As creatures they are linked to God through the act of creation. Yet, as creatures, they are also separated from God in their being mortal and rooted in the changes associated with temporality. The multitude of demons in the parable above occupy the individual human creature – that highest of creatures – and turn him into a mere animal-like thing. The iconography of the passage is striking – the true nature of the demons, we presume, is revealed by the choice of their receptacle in a herd of lowly beasts. But throughout the parable, the only real indication we have of this multitude of demons is this enigmatic resounding of the word "Legion." In a philosophical sense, that the demons choose to present themselves via voice and sound – at once present and absent – is noteworthy.

These two manifestations of the demon – the demons in the old man and the herd of animals – lead to a third type, which is the word-of-mouth among the people, which itself spreads like a disease. Jesus' demonstration of his sovereign and medical powers instills a certain horror in the people, resulting in his effectively being deported. We might take a decidedly modern view of this scene and suggest that the threat posed by the demons is not simply a topological one having to do with the proper relation between the One and the Many, and neither is it to do with the proper relation between Creator and creature. There is another element here, which is the way in which the demonic also challenges divine sovereignty. The demonic challenges the divine in its refusal to be organized at all. We do not know how many demons there are, nor even if it is more than one voice that speaks "Legion." We only know that it is more than one, and that it may be something other than "Many," the latter term still denoting a potentially countable entity. The demons are, in a sense, more than Many, but never One.

Examples of demonic activity occur throughout the New Testament, though in it demons are by no means represented in the same way. For example, the famous scene of the apocalypse in *Revelations* not only features a battle between angels and demons, but it also portrays avenging angels that tend to look a lot like demons. These supernatural creatures are anthropomorphized, and they even have their own technology: trumpets, tempests, and "bowls of plague" come forth in the apocalyptic upsurge. In these scenes the demons/angels have as their sole function a religious-juridical relation to the human (either to damn or to save them). The various symbolic devices, from scales and seals to bowls, are technologies for the end of the world. Here the demons are a form of *mediated presence*.

By contrast, the exorcism scene from the Gospels portrays a demon that is unmediated and yet only embodied – the demons called "Legion" are never present in themselves, but only via some form of earthly embodiment (the old man, the herd of pigs, the wind, the sea). In a sense, they are strangely pantheistic, announcing themselves only indirectly. Hence their embodiment is also a disembodiment, in the sense that they are wandering spirits – their movement happens more by demonic contagion than by divine inspiration. Demons are here a form of *immediate absence*.

While the anthropological meaning of the demon remains

ensconced within its human-centric, therapeutic solipsism (e.g. "why do we do the things we do?"), the mythological meaning focuses on the limits of the human ability to know the non-human. At its limit is the idea of the absolutely "dark" demon – the demon that remains absolutely unknowable to use as human beings, but which nevertheless seems to act upon us, perhaps through a malevolence we can only call "bad luck" or "misfortune."

RESPONSIO

If the anthropological demon is an attempt to reveal the nature of the human to the human, then we can say that the mythological demon is an attempt to reveal the non-human to the human. Both, however, come across certain limitations, due to the human point-of-view. The human is always relating either to itself or to the world. And these two types of relations overlap with each other: the human can only understand the human by transforming it into an object to relate to (psychology, sociology), while the human can only relate to the objective world itself by transforming the world into something familiar, accessible, or intuited in human terms (biology, geology, cosmology).

This leaves one avenue open, which is the perspective of the non-human itself. As thinking, embodied beings unable to fully detach ourselves from the subject-object relations that constitute us, this is undoubtedly a paradoxical move. In fact, it is doomed from the start. Nevertheless it deserves to be stated, even if beyond it there can only be silence. In the parable of the Gerasene demons, the demons named "Legion" were, in themselves, defined by several properties: they were neither One nor Many but somewhere in between; they were fully immanent with the world (almost pantheistically); and, most importantly, they in themselves were never present, never a discrete thing that one could point to – the demons named "Legion" were really, in themselves, "nothing."

Perhaps there is a meaning of the demonic that has little to do with the human at all – *and this indifference is what constitutes its demonic character*. If the anthropological demon (the human relating to itself) functioned via metaphor, and if the mythological demon (the human relating to the non-human) functioned via allegory, then perhaps there is a third demon, which is more ontological, or really "meontological" (having to do with non-being rather than being). As the 6th century mystic Dionysius the Areopagite notes, commenting on the paradoxical existence of demons, "evil is not a being; for if it were, it would not be totally evil...evil has no place among being."[6]

Given that, for us as human beings, there is no simple "going over" to the side of the non-human, it would seem that the mode best suited to this third type of demon is something like metonymy (with the demon as a stand-in for the abstract, indifferent, non-being of the world). The demon is, then, a way of talking about the perspective of the non-human, with all the contradictions this implies. For the meontological demon, affirmation is negation, and thinking about its being is the same as thinking about its non-being.

This is brought forward with great subtlety in Dante's *Inferno*, one of the classic depictions of the demonic. However, there is not simply one type of demon in the *Inferno*; indeed, the central drama of the *Inferno* is not good vs. evil, but in the tensions within the *Inferno* itself. For instance, one can identify at least three types of demons in the *Inferno*. First there is, at the center and lowest point of the underworld, the figure of Lucifer, the arch-demon. This takes place in the final scene of the *Inferno*, where Dante (who is both author and character in the story) is led by his guide Virgil to the center of the underworld. Dante (the author) uses the word Dis in the poem, an alternate name for Pluto, the god of the classical underworld, to refer to the giant, grotesque, brooding arch-emperor ("emperor of all these realms of gloom").

Here we have the counter-sovereign, who, like the divine sovereign, is centralized and transcendent with respect to that which he governs. However, this counter-sovereign demon actually does very little in the long journey that constitutes the *Inferno*. The 19th century artist Gustave Doré depicts the scene in great detail. Immobilized in the frozen waters of the underworld, this counter-sovereign demon is condemned to repeat the same cycle of transgression and blasphemy against the Creator.

Distinct from this, there are the multitude of demons found peppered throughout the different circles of the underworld. An example is the so-called Malebranche demons found in the 8th Circle. These are "demons" in the more modern, Faustian sense – they are torturers, tricksters, and tempters.

The Malebranche demons are less the giant, majestic counter-sovereign, and more a roving pack, a demonic gang. They operate according to the basic rules of the underworld, and are more decentralized, their power emanating from the rule of the counter-sovereign.

Contrasted to these two types of demons – the counter-sovereign Dis, and the Malebranche demons – there is a third, which comes near the beginning of the *Inferno*. This is in the Second Circle, the Circle of the Lustful. In a dramatic passage, Dante (the character) is lead by his guide Virgil to a precipice where, for the first time in the narrative, he encounters the strange and dark atmosphere of the demonic:

> I came to a place where no light shone at all,
> bellowing like the sea racked by a tempest,
> when warring winds attack it from both sides.

The infernal storm (*bufera infernal*), eternal in its rage,
sweeps and drives the spirits with its blast:
it whirls them, lashing them with punishment.

When they are swept back past their place of judgment,
then come the shrieks, laments, and anguished cries;
there they blaspheme God's almighty power.

To this place the lustful have been sent, all "those who make reason slave to appetite." The mass of bodies, blown back and forth by the wind, prompt a comparison to the swarming of birds:

and as the wings of starlings in the winter
bear them along in wide-spread, crowded flocks,
so does that wind propel the evil spirits (*spiriti mali*);

now here, then there, and up and down, it drives them
with never any hope to comfort them –
hope not of rest but even of suffering less.[7]

We soon learn that this tempestuous scene is not the backdrop for some new genre of demons, but that the wind, the rain, and the storm itself is the demon. This "black wind" (*aura nera*) is at once invisible and yet dramatically manifest, coursing through the swarming bodies of the damned.

One of the images from Doré's illustrations depicts the well-known scene in which two of the spirits – Paolo and Francesca – emerge from the swarm of bodies to tell their tale of tragic love. Dante the character, moved by the scene and their story, is overcome and faints next to Virgil, who is by his side. But what is equally interesting in the image is the way that Doré visually depicts the bodies of Paolo and Francesca: they barely stand out from the amorphous background of swarming spirits, which seem to recede back into infinity. Indeed, in certain areas the bodies appear to merge into the backdrop of the storm itself.

In this scene there is neither a fixed and majestic counter-sovereign, nor a roving gang of Faustian demons. There is only the strange, immanent, and fully distributed "life-force" of this black wind. The spirits of the Lustful in this circle dissolve into the elemental swarming of the storm and the wind. It is paradoxically the most manifest form of life (indeed, Dante the character faints before its force), and yet it is also the most empty (the demonic storm is not a discrete thing, much less a discrete body; it is everywhere but nowhere). Arguably, this last scene puts forth the most difficult view of the demon – not a transcendent, governing cause, and not an emanating, radiating flow – but a concept of the demonic that is fully immanent, and yet never fully present. This kind of demon is at once pure force and flow, but, not being a discrete thing in itself, it is also pure nothingness.

Generally speaking, the *Inferno* is of interest not simply due to the panoply of monsters that inhabit its pages, but because of the way in which it carefully stratifies different types of demonic being and non-being. Within the paths, rivers, caverns, and fortresses of the *Inferno* all boundaries collapse: there are human bodies melting into dead trees, rivers flowing with blood, and entire cities populated with the living dead. The motif of possession in the *Inferno* demonstrates this: demonic possession is not just the possession of living beings, but includes the possession of the non-living as well. Demons possess not only humans and animals, but also the very landscape, the very terrain of the underworld. Demonic possession in the *Inferno* is not just teratological, but also geological and even climatological.

QUÆSTIO III – On Demonology, and Whether it is a Respectable Field of Study

ARTICULUS

Demonology is commonly understood to no longer be of contemporary relevance; it is an unfortunate and anachronistic offshoot of late Medieval and early Renaissance theology, the stuff of the imaginative fancy of modern horror films. However, recent work by scholars such as Alain Bourreau, Nancy Caciola, Stuart Clark, and Armando Maggi, has done much to tease out the philosophical and political aspects of demonology in its historical sense. The term "demonology" itself is most often understood as the study and classification of demons (often inclusive of activities such as witchcraft and necromancy), directly tied to the long, dark history of the witch-hunts and persecutions of heretics in Europe between the 15th-17th centuries. While Christian theologians from Augustine to Aquinas had written extensively about the nature of evil prior to this period, the idea that a distinct field of study devoted to the topic – as well as to its practical application in combating and rooting out evil – does not really emerge until the late 15th century. An often-cited reference point is the papal bull *Summis Desiderantes Affectibus* (1484), issued by Pope Innocent VIII in response to growing concerns that heretical activities, including witchcraft, constituted a serious threat to the unification of Church authority across the continent. The bull is noteworthy for several reasons, the foremost being that it confirmed the existence of witches, witchcraft, and the activities of all those who "have abandoned themselves to demons," through rituals undertaken "at the instigation of the Enemy of Mankind." If identifying an enemy as an enemy is to give that enemy strength, then this identification of witchcraft and demonic dealings would prove to be a double-edged sword. Of the countless trials and executions that took place under the banner of the Inquisition (modern estimates by historians range from 40,000 to 100,000 executions in continental Europe alone, between 1500-1700), the scope of the witch-trials broadened, in some cases including the mere defense against an accusation of witchcraft as itself constituting an act of heresy.

The bull *Summis Desiderantes Affectibus* not only identified a threat, it also made recommendations for dealing with that threat. It gave Church inquisitors such as Heinrich Kramer and Jacob Sprenger the authority to legally seek out, put to trial, and to punish those suspected of dealing with demons and practicing witchcraft. Roughly two years after the publication of the bull, Kramer and Sprenger published the book that would become the blueprint for the witch-hunt manual: the *Malleus Maleficarum* (*Hammer of Witches*, 1486). Much of the *Malleus Maleficarum* is typical of the writing on witchcraft and demonology of the period. There are references to the writings of the Church Fathers and Scholastic theologians on the dangers of evil and evil-doing demons. There are also attempts to distinguish and classify the different kinds of demonic activity. And there are a number of case studies of witchcraft, demonic possession, and other acts of *malefica* that serve to paint a picture of the real threat at hand.

What makes the *Malleus Maleficarum* unique, however, is its practical orientation. It is not a work of theological speculation, as is Aquinas's *De Malo* (*On Evil*, ca. 1270). Neither is it an attempt at systematic classification, as is Francesco-Maria Guazzo's *Compendium Maleficarum* (*Encyclopedia of Witchcraft*, 1608). It is, quite literally, an instruction manual, clearly demonstrated by the book's three parts: Part I, which argues that witches and witchcraft really exist, and are a threat; Part II, which deals with how witches and witchcraft can be detected and exposed; and Part III, which outlines the protocols for carrying out the trial, sentencing, and punishment or execution.

Of particular interest is the role played by 16th century medicine in demonology manuals like the *Malleus Maleficarum*. One role medicine played was in the cultivation of a general miasmatic or contagion-theory of demonic possession. In this pre-modern understanding of contagion, the demon is conceptualized in much the same way we saw earlier – as a paradoxical manifestation that is, in itself, "nothing" or non-being. This is illustrated in the *Malleus Maleficarum* by the three main types of demonic possession, each exhibiting anomalous symptoms that – in the argument of the demonologist – can be causally traced to some sort of commerce with a demon. At the first level there is psycho-physiological possession, in which the demonic spirit invades and affects the body itself (with symptoms ranging from temporary disability and incapacitation, to impotence, infertility, and eroto-mania, to epilepsy, narcolepsy, and melancholia). At a second level there are cases of epidemiological possession, which affects the relation between body and environment (plague, leprosy, mass hysteria, even mob behavior). Finally, at a third level one finds a more abstract, climatological possession, in which demons possess not only the living but the non-living, not only the animate but the inanimate (unnatural or anomalous changes in weather, affected livestock or crops, sudden famine or flood).

Added to this epistemological role of medicine is another role, which is juridical. Though the *Malleus Maleficarum* is a decidedly single-minded text, aiming without hesitation at the extermination of all witchcraft activity, it does make minimal allowances for natural, as opposed to supernatural, causes of witchcraft (that are in no way less punishable). While there was rarely any question as to the supernatural character of the witch or witchcraft activity in question, the exact cause of the said activity could be open to interpretation. There may be, for example, a supernatural cause producing a natural symptom. Such symptoms could be classified as either illusion or illness. If illusion, then the question was whether the accused is intentionally using some sort of trickery, and for what reason (e.g. gain of money, revenge, jealousy, etc.). If illness, then the question was what type of illness, the most commonly-cited examples being the vaguely-defined illnesses of epilepsy, hysteria, and melancholy.. The role of medicine here was less to develop knowledge about demonic possession, and more to arbitrate – within the juridical context of the trial – the boundary between the natural and supernatural. Interestingly, it is this role that would be reinforced by later writers more skeptical of the witch-hunts and the mass paranoia they produced. Note, however, that a natural explanation of a phenomenon such as necromancy or possession in no way rules out the presence of the supernatural – in many instances it simply serves as yet another route towards the inevitable sentence.

Although witch-hunting manuals proliferated throughout the period, the *Malleus Maleficarum* set a new standard, encompassing theology (Part I), medicine (Part II), and law (Part III) into a single work. The result was not only a new set of juridical procedures, but also a new discourse and way of thinking about the demon in terms of the non-human. This is also evident in the early Renaissance debates over the status of demons and demonic possession, in treatises such as Johann Weyer's *De Praestigiis Daemonium* (*On the Trickery of Demons*, 1563), Jean Bodin's *Démonomanie des Sorciers* (*The Demon-mania of Witches*, 1580), and Reginald Scot's *Discoverie of Witchcraft* (1584).

Weyer's *De Praestigiis Daemonium* is noteworthy for being one of the few treatises that expresses criticism of the excesses of the with-hunts and witchcraft trials. While Weyer did admit the real existence of witches, witchcraft, and demons, he also allowed for cases in which individuals were helplessly deluded by demons (thinking that their hallucinations were real), as well as cases of simple trickery. As Weyer ominously notes, real demons do not need us to carry out their acts of ill will – in fact, it is the height of vanity to suppose that we as human beings are in any way necessary for them. Be that as it may, it is noteworthy that Weyer, who studied under the scientist and reputed magician Cornelius Agrippa, spent most of his life as a physician, and this impacts his allowance for medical-psychological explanations of witchcraft. He notes, with biting sarcasm, that "such rare and severe symptoms often arise in diseases that stem from natural causes but are immediately attributed to witchcraft by men of no scientific experience and little faith."[8] *De Praestigiis Daemonium* also contains a number of indictments against the excessive use of torture and maltreatment of accused witches – at least before a proper examination of a case can be carried out.

Bodin's *Démonomanie* is a direct counter-attack to Weyer. Bodin, a Carmelite monk, member of Parliament, and professor of law, is mostly known in political philosophy for his massive work *Les Six Livres de la République*, a work which contains an early theorization of absolute state sovereignty. Written in order to aid judges in witchcraft cases, Bodin's *Démonomanie* is a disturbing work that advocates, among other things, the legal use of torture to elicit confessions of guilt, including the use of techniques such as cautery. It also contains one of the early legal definitions of a witch, as one whom "knowing God's law, tries to bring about some act through an agreement with the Devil." It also contains a veritable litany of the anti-human antagonism of demons: "...all demons are malevolent, deceiving, posturing enemies of humanity..."[9] The *Démonomanie* never wavers in its assertion of the religious and political threat of witchcraft – that is, the threat that witchcraft posed to statecraft. The conviction in the *Démonomanie* appears to derive in part from Bodin's own experience as a judge, in which he saw a number of witchcraft trials (and purportedly showed no hesitation in torturing children and invalids to gain a confession).

If Weyer represents the attitude of temperance towards witchcraft (under the guise of medicine), and if Bodin represents the conservative retrenchment (under the guise of law), then Scot's *Discoverie of Witchcraft* takes the next step, which is to question the validity of the entire affair altogether. To the role of medicine in Weyer, and the role of law in Bodin, we have the role of skepticism in Scot. While Weyer and Bodin are on opposite sides of the fence politically, theologically they both remain committed to the existence of supernatural forces and the conflict paradigm of good vs. evil. Scot, who had the advantage of relative financial independence, was neither beholden to the Church nor to science in his opinions – though the *Discoverie of Witchcraft* was printed at his own expense, was unregistered, and did not contain the publisher's name. Most likely spurred on by a series of controversial witch trials in England in the early 1580s, Scot's treatise is much more sarcastic, even humorous, in its criticisms. He attacks both the pretenses of witches and witchcraft, dismissing them as trickery (either on others or on oneself), as well as the "extreme and intolerable tyranny" of the inquisitors and judges. In a sense, Scot's treatise is a sort of clearing-house for the very concept of the demon, and indeed of the supernatural itself. As if to accuse both witches and inquisitors of a too-provincial, all-too-human mindset, the *Discoverie of Witchcraft* suggests that, in so far as there is a concept of the demon, it has to be one of which we can have little or no knowledge.

SED CONTRA

The debates surrounding witchcraft and demonology are instructive in that they often revolve around our ability to adequately comprehend the supernatural – be it divine or demonic. In particular, the question of the demon tends to oscillate, from highly anthropomorphic Satyrs to the more abstract and obscure demons that contagiously pass in the breath from person to person. Much of the confusion of the early demonology treatises centers on how to verify the existence of a demon, when, by definition, they are rarely self-evident to the human observer. In cases where demonic possession cannot be distinguished from medical illness, on which side should one stand? To the 21st century mind, the question is absurd. But for an era in which the lines between magic, science, and witchcraft were blurry, such questions were not only religious and political, but philosophical too. To the culture of the early Renaissance, the demon presents a limit to the empiricism of the unknown, something that can only be verified through contradictions – an absent manifestation, an unnatural creature, a demonic malady.

Such contradictions stretch the limits of language. Indeed, one of the by-products of the flurry of writings on demonology was the development of a new language and a new set of concepts for thinking about the supernatural. Certainly this language and these concepts were informed by theology, but, in describing the effects of possession, in evoking the scene of the witches' Sabbath, and in imagining a world swarming with malefic entities, a certain *poetics* of the demon was also needed. Demonology – whether it aims to convince or to criticize – is as much a rhetorical activity as it is a theological or juridical one. Thus, in contrast to the view of demonology as theological, we can briefly consider a poetics as being equally central to the concept of the demon.

If one were to outline a poetics of the demon, one could begin by thinking about the demonic in literary representations. More specifically, one could understand the demon as represented via different motifs. For example the narrative technique of the journey – so common in the history of world literature – is a key feature of Dante's *Commedia,* as Dante the pilgrim journeys from the dark circles of Hell, through the conical spiral of Purgatory, to the celestial geometries of Paradise, along the way under-going various trials of his own. This is a topological motif, in which we encounter various people, places, and creatures. The demonic is here symbolically inscribed by a particular locale (for instance, the way that the different circles of Hell contain different classes of demonic punishments for different sins).

The same follows for other narrative motifs. There is the battle, such as one finds in Milton's *Paradise Lost,* and, following upon (and critiquing) Milton, as one finds in scenes from William Blake's prophecies. Here we find the structure of agonism, with the demonic ensnared in an eternal struggle or conflict. Then there is the motif of the pact, the black bargain with a demon that at once liberates and imprisons the human character that signs their name in blood. This is a juridical and economic structure, most commonly associated with the Faust story and its literary incarnations by such authors as Marlowe and Goethe – I give you my soul, and in exchange, you give me...everything. The pact often overlaps with another narrative motif, which is that of the ritual. The infamous depictions of the Black Mass in novels such as Huysmans' *Là-bas* or Dennis Wheatley's *The Devil Rides Out* involve a whole series of sacrile-gious acts that, at the same time, express a sanctity of evil. The demonic is the counter-divine, at once negating the divine while sanctifying the demonic. Wheatley's "black" novels are particularly noteworthy, for the protagonist De Richleau often uses both ancient and modern-scientific knowledge in his battle against demons and dark forces, continuing the "occult detective" genre inaugurated by authors such as Sheridan Le Fanu. Finally, there is the more modern, technological motif of the magical artifact, the dark invention that signals a new kind of apocalypse. Science fiction works such as Fritz Leiber's *Gather, Darkness!* and James Blish's *Faust Aleph-Null*, written in the shadow of world war and mass extinction, suggest a ominous affinity between technology and the supernatural. In Leiber's novel a futuristic Papacy utilizes a panoply of special-effects technologies to ensure the fidelity of the masses to the hegemony of the Church. Against them a demonic underworld of witches, warlocks, and familiars carry out their revolutionary cause. By contrast, Blish's novel suggests that with weapons of mass destruction, a renewed Faustian pact has been made, with quantum physics as a form of necromancy. In these 20th century works, the demonic plays different roles, either as a revolutionary counter-power, or as an essentially unknowable force beyond human comprehension and human control.

One of the striking commonalities between works of this type is that nearly all of them seem to follow an unwritten rule – the demonic antagonist must always "lose" in the end. Certainly this would seem to follow the moral structure of the novel or the epic poem (similar to the requisite happy ending of a studio film). But one always feels a little let down by this *deus ex machina*. Goethe's Faust goes all the way in his demonic explorations, only to later repent and – in Part II – gain salvation by virtue of divine grace. Similarly there is Blake's famous statement about Milton's *Paradise Lost* – that the latter was of the Devil's party without knowing it. Here one finds the problem of "being-on-the-side-of" the demonic, when the demonic is unknown and, perhaps, unknowable. However, the failure of the demonic antagonists in literary examples like these is perhaps less a testament to the victorious nature of good, and more an indication of a certain moral economy of the unknown. By the end of Goethe's *Faust* we know no more or less of the demonic than when we started, in spite of having the wool pulled over our eyes.

RESPONSIO

Here again we arrive at the concept of the demon as a limit for thought, a limit that is constituted not by being or becoming, but by non-being, or nothingness. And here we should state what we have been hinting at all along, which is that in contrast to the theology of the demon, or the poetics of the demon, there is something more basic still that has to do with the ideas of negation and nothingness – hence we should really think of the demon as an ontological problem (not theology, not poetry, but philosophy).

True, demonology is a theological phenomenon, tied up with historical debates about the nature of evil, and the politics surrounding the witch-hunts. True, demonology is also a cultural phenomenon, as the poetic, literary, cinematic, and video game examples demonstrate. But demonology ceases to be interesting if it is taken as being "merely" historical, or "only" a fiction. If demonology is to be thought in a philo-sophical register, then it would have to function as a kind of philosoheme that brings together a cluster of ideas that have, for some time, served as problematic areas for philosophy itself: negation, nothingness, and the non-human.

What would such an approach to demonology look like? To begin with, demonology would have to be distinguished from anthropology, in which the demon is simply a stand-in for the human and ruminations on the nature of evil in human beings. Demonology would also have to be distinguished from pure metaphysics, in which the demon functions as a stand-in for the pair being/non-being. Denying the anthropological view means considering the world as not simply the world-for-us or the world-in-itself, but as the world-without-us. Likewise denying the view of metaphysics means considering the unreliability of the principle of sufficient reason for thinking about the world (not sufficient reason but a strange, uncanny, insufficiency of reason). A philosophical demonology would therefore have to be "against" the human being – both the "human" part as well as the "being" part.

Perhaps we can come up with a new term for this way of thinking – *demontology*. If anthropology is predicated on a division between the personal and the impersonal ("man" and cosmos), then a demontology collapses them into paradoxical pairings (impersonal affects, cosmic suffering). If ontology deals with the minimal relation being/non-being, then demontology would have to undertake the thought of nothingness (a negative definition), but a nothingness that is also not simply non-being (a privative definition). Schopenhauer provides an explanation, recapping his distinction between the two kinds of negation:

> I must first of all observe that the concept of *nothing* (*Nichts*) is essentially relative, and always refers to a definite something that it negates. This quality has been attributed (especially by Kant) merely to the *nihil privativum* indicated by – in contrast to +. This negative sign (–) from the opposite point of view might become +, and, in opposition to this *nihil privativum*, the *nihil negativum* has been set up, which would in every respect be nothing...But considered more closely, an absolute nothing, a really proper *nihil negativum*, is not even conceivable, but everything of this kind, considered from a higher standpoint or subsumed under a wider concept, is always only a *nihil privativum*.[10]

For Schopenhauer, the *nihil privativum* is the world as it appears to us, the world-for-us, the world as "Representation"

(*Vorstellung*), while the *nihil negativum* is the world-in-itself or the world as "Will" – or better, the world-in-itself as it is manifest to us in its inaccessibility, in its enigmatic, "occult qualities." As Schopenhauer notes, "what is universally assumed as positive, what we call *being* (*Seiende*), the negation of which is expressed by the concept *nothing* (*Nichts*) in its most general significance, is exactly the world as representation."[11] As for the other path, the *nihil negativum*, Schopenhauer – who is otherwise vociferous in his attacks on religion – suggests a strange affinity with mysticism:

> But so long as we ourselves are the will-to-live, this last, namely the nothing as that which exists, can be known and expressed by us only negatively...If, however, it should be absolutely insisted on that somehow a positive knowledge is to be acquired of what philosophy can express only negatively as denial of the will, nothing would be left but to refer to that state which is experienced by all who have attained to complete denial of the will, and which is denoted by the names ecstasy, rapture, illumination, union with God, and so on.[12]

In a sense, the *nihil negativum* is not just about the limits of language to adequately describe experience; it is about the horizon of thought as it confronts the unthought, the horizon of the human as it struggles to comprehend the unhuman. Yet, as Schopenhauer notes, "such a state cannot really be called knowledge, since it no longer has the form of subject and object; moreover, it is accessible only to one's own experience that cannot be further communicated."[13]

Given this distinction (the *nihil privativum* and the *nihil negativum*), and its implications for thinking the world as a non-human world, we are led to a dilemma. That is, a demontology of the type we've been discussing would have to distinguish itself from the moral, juridical, and cosmic framework of Christian demonology (moral law, temptation, transgression, sin, punishment, salvation, etc.). And here demontology comes up against one of the greatest challenges for thought today, and it is, in many ways, a Nietzschean one – how does one rethink the world as unthinkable? – that is, in the absence of the human-centric point of view, and without an over-reliance on the metaphysics of being?

Again, we run up against all sorts of obstacles, in part because a philosophical demonology does not exist – or not yet. Should one then create a lineage, citing predecessors of this type of Cosmic Pessimism? But here an interminable game of inclusion and exclusion begins. Should one include classical philosophers, such as Heraclitus? Should one include works in the tradition of "darkness mysticism" or negative theology? And then what of the great works of spiritual and philosophical crisis, from Kierkegaard to Emil Cioran and Simone Weil? We've already mentioned Schopenhauer and Nietzsche, but then are we obliged to also consider their 20th century inheritors, such as Bataille, Klossowski, or Shestov? Then again, would there not be a basic problem in positing or hoping for the existence of a field dedicated to negation and nothingness? Is it possible for one to make the claim that demontology exists, without becoming ensnared in an endless theater of the absurd? Perhaps the only thing for certain is if something like a demontology could exist, it would not be made any more respectable because of its existence – for nothing is more frowned upon than nothing...

II. Six *Lectio* on Occult Philosophy

Preamble: On Agrippa's *De Occulta Philosophia*

The phrase "occult philosophy" is often used by scholars to describe an intellectual movement prevalent during the Renaissance, which combined elements of Christian theology with a range of non-Christian traditions, from ancient Egyptian theories of magic to Renaissance astronomy and alchemy. In its own way, occult philosophy's mashing of diverse intellectual traditions questioned the hegemony of any one particular tradition (most notably, orthodox Christianity as ensconced within a whole host of legal documents defining the parameters of heresy). In our increasing awareness of the cataclysmic effects of climate change and global warming, and yet after the "death of God," what new meanings can occult philosophy have today?

Occult philosophy is first and foremost a historical phenomenon. Modern work by scholars such as Frances Yates has done much to place occult philosophy within its philosophical, religious, and political context. In her book *The Occult Philosophy in the Elizabethan Age*, Yates argues that what has come to be called occult philosophy is really an amalgam of diverse intellectual traditions, traditions that have, historically speaking, often been at odds with each other. In this mixing together of different speculative traditions, one finds: Greek natural philosophy (Aristotle) and cosmology (Pythagoras), Neoplatonism, Renaissance alchemy, Egyptian Hermeticism, Christian-Scholastic theology, and Jewish mysticism. The work of Heinrich Cornelius Agrippa, in particular, stands out for its eclecticism and its ambitious attempt to synthesize diverse philosophical and theological traditions. In Agrippa's work, Yates identifies a thread that combines Hermeticism, as filtered through Renaissance thinkers such as Marsilio Ficino, and a hybrid Christian-Cabbalistic mysticism as filtered through thinkers such as Giovanni Pico della Mirandola. However, in Yates' view, Agrippa's text takes occult philosophy in directions that other thinkers were not prepared to go, for fear of accusations of heresy. "It is the Ficinian magic which Agrippa teaches in his first book, though he teaches it in a much bolder way. Ficino was nervous of the magic; he was anxious to keep his magic 'natural,' concerned only with elemental substances in their relations to the stars and avoiding the 'star demons,' the spirits connected with the stars. It was really not possible to teach astral magic whilst avoiding the star demons, as Agrippa saw and boldly accepted the challenge."[14]

First published in 1531, Agrippa's *De Occulta Philosophia Libri Tres* (*Three Books of Occult Philosophy*) presents a veritable compendium of Renaissance philosophy, theology, mysticism, science, and magic. While Agrippa began writing the *Occult Philosophy* as early as 1509, the work itself went through a number of editions, with an English translation appearing in 1651. An itinerant scholar, Agrippa traveled extensively throughout Europe, coming into contact with intellectuals participating in the religious reform and scientific humanism movements of the time (some modern historians even suggest that Agrippa's travels point to an unknown secret society of which he was a member). The *Occult Philosophy* has had a tremendous impact on later generations, its influence seen in the 19th century European revival of occultism (for instance, in the work of Eliphas Lévi or Gérard Encausse in France) and in early 20th century groups such as the Golden Dawn and the Theosophical Society.

In Agrippa's philosophy, the nature of reality is divided into three worlds – the elemental world, the celestial world, and the intellectual world. Each of these terms has specific meanings in the context of Renaissance occult philosophy. By "elemental" Agrippa means the natural world, comprising as it does the spectrum of animate and inanimate entities, organic and inorganic nature, as well as the primary elements as inherited from classical thought (water, air, fire, and earth). Beyond the elemental or natural world is what Agrippa calls the "celestial," by which he means the sky, the stars, the firmament, and the planetary cosmos. This celestial domain is partially that as defined within the science of astronomy, and partially that as defined within the long tradition of Neoplatonic cosmology, Pythagoreanism, and Cabbalistic mysticism. Finally, beyond the celestial is the "intellectual" world, and here Agrippa displays again the influence of Neoplatonism, referring to the super-natural world of intermediary beings (angels and demons) as well as the First Cause, the Neoplatonic "One," or God. Hence "intellectual" has little relation to the modern, colloquial sense of the cognitive functions of the brain. This last world is intel-lectual in the sense that it contains, in Platonic fashion, the abstract, purely formal essence of all things in the celestial and elemental worlds.

The philosophical commitment of Agrippa's *Occult Philosophy* is that there is a basic distinction between the world as its appears to us, and the "hidden" or occulted qualities of the world which, though they are not apparent, are all the more important and essential in gaining a deeper knowledge of the three worlds (elemental, celestial, intellectual). While most of the *Occult Philosophy* is dedicated to detailing, often in a very practical way, the process of revealing the hidden essences of the world, the world as such doesn't always lend itself to being revealed. In fact, there are a number of moments in the text that describe the world as in fact refusing to be revealed at all. Early on in the first book, Agrippa includes a number of interesting chapters on what he calls the "occult virtues of things." The strange effects of certain herbs or minerals, anomalies in the sky or the stars, the practice of necromancy or geomancy, even the existence of magic itself – all these are evidence of aspects of the world that refuse to reveal themselves, that remain hidden or occulted. As Agrippa notes, "they are called occult qualities, because their causes lie hid, and man's intellect cannot in any way reach, and find them out."[15] His examples vary widely, from the mundane example of how digestion occurs, to the rather fantastical example of how creatures such as satyrs may exist. All these examples are united by their existing and yet being unexplainable by human beings: "So there are in things, besides the elementary qualities which we know, other certain innate virtues created by nature, which we admire, and are amazed at, being such as we know not, and indeed seldom or never have seen."[16]

This idea – of the occulted world which both makes its presence known and yet in so doing reveals to us the unknown – this idea is the dark underside of occult philosophy and its humanist claims. Against the humanist world-for-us, a human-centric world made in our image, there is this notion of the world as occulted, not in a relative but in an absolute sense. Etymologically speaking, that which is "occult" (*occultus*; *occulere*) is something hidden, concealed, and surrounded by shadows. However, that which is hidden implies that which is revealed (*revelare*), just as that which is already apparent may, by some twist, suddenly become obscure and occult. That which is occulted can be hidden in a number of ways: something can intentionally be hidden, as when a precious object or important piece of information is stored away or withheld (buried treasures or best-kept secrets). In this case we enter the human world of hide-and-seek, of giving and withholding, of all the micro-exchanges of power that constitute human social networks. We as human beings actively hide and reveal things that, by virtue of this hiding and revealing activity, obtain a certain value for us as knowledge.

To this we can add another way in which the occult is hidden, and that is a hiddenness in which we as human beings play little or no part, and which is either already given, or which occurs in spite of, or indifferently to, our attempts to reveal that which is hidden. This second type of hiddenness – which may be cataclysmic or everyday – is the hiddenness of the world that we find ourselves thrown into, a hidden world which, regardless of how much knowledge we produce about it, always retains some remainder that lies beyond the scope of our capacity to reveal its hiddenness. In some cases the hidden world is simply the world that does not bend to our will or to our desires, the differential between the world as the world-for-us and the world as the world-in-itself. In other cases the hidden world may be something like the "unsolved mysteries" that percolate in our popular culture fascination of the paranormal.

Let us introduce a terminology for talking about the occult in a contemporary context. This second notion of the occult – not that which we as human being hide or reveal, but that which is already hidden in the world – this we can refer to simply as the occulted world, or better, the *hiddenness of the world*. But here we need to make a further refinement. The hiddenness of the world is not just the world-in-itself, for the world-in-itself is, by definition, absolutely cut off from us as human beings in the world (the world-for-us). When the world-in-itself becomes occulted, or "hidden," a strange and paradoxical movement takes place whereby the world-in-itself presents itself to us, but without ever becoming fully accessible or completely knowable. The world-in-itself presents itself to us, but without simply becoming the world-for-us; it is, to borrow from Schopenhauer, "the world-in-itself-for-us."

If this is the case – that the world-in-itself paradoxically presents itself to us – then what is it exactly that is presented, what is revealed? Quite simply, what is revealed is the "hiddenness" of the world, in itself (and not, I stress, the world-in-itself). This hiddenness is also, in a way, hideous. The hidden world, which reveals nothing other than its hiddenness, is a blank, anonymous world that is indifferent to human knowledge, much less to our all-too-human wants and desires. Hence the hiddenness of the world, in its anonymity and indifference, is a world for which the idea of a theistic providence or the scientific principle of sufficient reason, are both utterly insufficient.

With this in mind, we can suggest a new approach to "occult philosophy" as defined by Agrippa. Whereas in traditional occult philosophy, the world is hidden in order that it is revealed (and revealed as the world-for-us), in occult philosophy today the world simply reveals its hiddenness to us. A second shift follows from this. Whereas traditional occult philosophy is a hidden knowledge of the open world, occult philosophy today is an open knowledge of the hiddenness of the world. Despite Agrippa's criticisms of both science and religion, the orientation of his work remains within the ambit of Renaissance humanism. For Agrippa it is not only possible for humanity to gain knowledge of the world, but it is also possible for humanity to, by virtue of occult practices, obtain a higher "union" with the "Maker of all things." Today, in an era almost schizophrenically poised between religious fanaticisms and a mania for scientific hegemony, all that remains is the hiddenness of the world, its impersonal "resistance" to the human *tout court*. Hence, in traditional occult philosophy knowledge is hidden, whereas in occult philosophy today the world is hidden, and, in the last instance, only knowable in its hiddenness. This implies a third shift, which is the following: whereas traditional occult philosophy is historically rooted in Renaissance humanism, the new occult philosophy is anti-humanist, having as its method the revealing of the non-human as a limit for thought...

What follows are a series of informal readings, or *lectio*, which trace this theme of occult philosophy and the hiddenness of the world. In Medieval philosophy and theology, a *lectio* (literally, a "reading") is a meditation on a particular text that can serve as a jumping-off point for further ideas. Traditionally the texts were scriptural, and the *lectio* would be delivered orally akin to a modern-day lecture; the *lectio* could also vary in form from shorter more informal meditations (*lectio brevior*) to more elaborate textual exegeses (*lectio difficilior*). We begin with a first group of *lectio* (*lectio* 1-3) that depict the use of the magic circle in literature. Here the motif of the magic circle serves as a boundary between the natural and supernatural, and the possible mediations between them that are made possible by the circle itself. Hence the magic circle is not only a boundary, but also a passage, a gateway, a portal. In these cases the hidden world reveals itself at the same time that it recedes into darkness and obscurity (hence the tragic tone of many of these stories). The second group of *lectio* (*lectio* 4-6) will take this motif in another direction, asking what happens when the hidden world reveals itself without any magic circle to serve as boundary. Here blobs, slime, ooze, mists, and clouds are prevalent, being not quite pure nature and yet not quite pure supernature. This moment – the manifestation of the hidden world without boundaries or mediation – will lead us to ask whether there is a new kind of "political theology" on the horizon, one that ambivalently attempts to manage this age-old boundary between the natural and supernatural.

1. Marlowe's *The Tragedy of Doctor Faustus* ~ Goethe's *Faust I*

In his study of the cultural anthropology of play, Johan Huizinga notes how play involves a number of ritualized practices, in which play is at once separated from the everyday world and yet mirrors it and comments upon it. The games we play, whether as children or as adults, at once reaffirm hegemonic social structures while also revealing to us the rules of play. Whether they are games of chance or games of strategy, play achieves this ambivalence through a spatial and symbolic motif that Huizinga calls "the magic circle." As Huizinga notes, "play moves and has its being within a play-ground marked off beforehand either materially or ideally, deliberately or as a matter of course."[17]

The magic circle need not actually be a circle, nor need it be magical. "Just as there is no formal difference between play and ritual, so the 'consecrated spot' cannot be formally distinguished from the play-ground." Hence a playing field, a game board, or even a special hall or building can be an incarnation of the magic circle: "The arena, the card-table, the magic circle, the temple, the stage, the screen, the tennis court, the court of justice, etc., all are in form and function play-grounds, i.e. forbidden spots, isolated, hedged round, hallowed, within which special rules obtain."[18]

Despite this everydayness – or indeed because of it – Huizinga notes that the "circle as such, however, has a magic significance."[19] For Huizinga, the magic circle has its roots in classical world mythology, in which one finds the themes of fate and free will at the hands of the gods or cosmic forces. Huizinga notes that in the *Mahābhārata*, for instance, a game of dice is played among the descendents of the legendary king Kuru. The place where the game is played "is a simple circle, *dyūtaman-dalam*, drawn on the ground…The players are not allowed to leave the ring until they have discharged all their obligations."[20]

Hence the magic circle has a cosmological significance, mirroring the cosmic or mythic ordering of the universe. This is inseparable from a social and political significance, in which the magic circle delimits a boundary between law and transgression, the legitimate and illegitimate, the sacred and profane. All incarnations of the magic circle "are temporary worlds within the ordinary world, dedicated to the performance of an act apart."[21]

One of the most noteworthy uses of the magic circle is in the form of ritual magic, particularly as it applies to the literary representations of necromancy and demonology. These instances are not only literal uses of a magic circle, but they also demonstrate, in their successes or failures, the political and theological aspects of the magic circle that historians such as Huizinga point out. The Faust myth provides one example. Though there are at least one or more historical personages known as Faust, little is known of their lives except by hearsay.

In 16th century Germany, several books recounting the life of Faust were in circulation. These "Faustbooks," as they are known, detail the basic elements of the story: Faust's challenge to faith, his pact with a demon, and his eventual downfall and damnation. One Faustbook tells how Faust, after dismissing the miracles performed by Christ, began to demonstrate his ability to perform miracles just as easily. When confronted by the Church, Faust rebukes, noting that "I have gone further than you think and have pledged myself to the devil with my own blood, to be his in eternity. How, then, can I return? Or how could I be helped?"[22]

In the late 16th century Faustbooks began to be translated and made their way around the continent. In England *The Damnable Life and Deserved Death of Dr. John Faustus* was published around 1588. It is thought that this edition prompted the playwright Christopher Marlowe to compose the first version of his own Faust story, *The Tragical History of Doctor*

Faustus in 1604. Marlowe's version of the Faust myth is noteworthy for several reasons. It formalizes with great detail the ritual practices of Faust, while also raising a host of difficult theological and philosophical questions regarding the mobile boundary between science and religion. In Marlowe's first edition, the play opens with a despondent Faustus questioning and then abandoning all (legitimate) forms of human knowledge as limited and inefficacious: "Bid *On kai me on* farewell. Galen, come! / Seeing *ubi desinit philosophus, ibi incipit medicus,* / Be a physician, Faustus. Heap up gold, / And be eternized for some wondrous cure."[23] Showing off his classical education, Marlowe has Faustus almost indifferently rattle off Greek and Latin – he bids farewell to *On kai me on* or the question of being and not-being so central to Greek philosophy; he then takes up the proverb *ubi desinit philosophus, ibi incipit medicus,* or "where the philosopher ends, the physician begins," announcing his intent to move beyond theory and into practice.

What is left for Faustus to do, seeing that all human knowledge has come to naught for him? Should he turn to religion? Here Faustus expresses his most vitriolic phrases, for with religion "We deceive ourselves" in an absurd, vicious circle of temptation, sin, and repentance – thus Faustus claims, "Divinity, adieu!"[24] In Marlowe's version, all that is left are the dark arts. As Faustus picks up an unnamed book of magic, he notes how "These metaphysics of magicians / And necromantic books are heavenly, / Lines, circles, signs, letters, and characters - / Ay, these are those that Faustus most desires."[25] This litany of magical tools – "lines, circles, signs, letters, and characters" – already paves the way for Faustus' use of the magic circle in his evocation of demons, the act that has come to define the Faust myth.

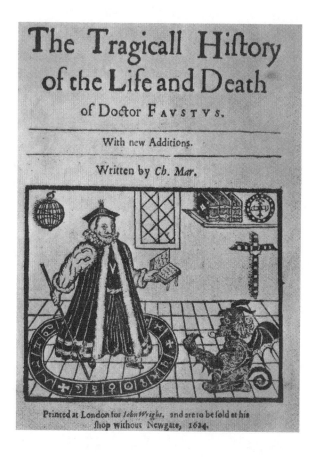

The key scene appears in both versions of the play, though in the second version of 1616 both the stage directions and the changes in the text create a much more dramatic, even cataclysmic atmosphere. The second version begins with thunder and a storm. We see Faustus in his study, with his books of black magic. Suspended above him is a swarm of demons, including Lucifer. Faustus is unaware that they are there, suspended above him, but we in the audience can see them, waiting. The ritual is worth citing in full, particularly for the way that it connects Faustus' use of the magic circle with elemental and even planetary forces:

Now that the gloomy shadow of the night,
Longing to view Orion's drizzling look,
Leaps from th'Antarctic world unto the sky
And dims the welkin with her pitchy breath,
Faustus, begin thine incantations,
And try if devils will obey thy hest,
Seeing thou hast prayed and sacrificed to them
[He draws a circle]
Within this circle is Jehovah's name
Forward and backward anagrammatized,
Th'abbreviated names of holy saints,
Figures of every adjunct to the heavens,
And characters of signs and erring stars,
By which the spirits are enforced to rise.
Then fear not, Faustus, to be resolute,
And try the utmost magic can perform.[26]

Following this we get more thunder and Faust incanting in Latin his evocation. The demon Mephistopheles appears, and the two begin their dialogue that eventually leads Faustus to sign in blood the pact with the demon. However, what is striking in the passage above is the way in which the "hidden world" of occult philosophy appears to suddenly and cataclysmically become revealed. Planets shift, winds howl, and a demon emerges from the smoke – this is, to be sure, the stuff of contemporary horror film. Yet for all this spectacle, the world, by the play's end, remains shadowy and hidden, up to the final scenes where Faustus is dragged into the underworld as fulfillment of the pact.

What is also interesting is that Marlowe brings together two shadowy bodies of knowledge of the Elizabethan era: that of occult philosophy and its connections between the microcosm and macrocosm, and that of the ongoing controversies over and persecutions of witchcraft and demonology. Both discourses raise a topic hotly debated among theologians and law-makers of the time, principally, the relation between the natural and the supernatural, or between the "scientific" cosmology of the planets and elements, and the "religious" topology of angels, demons, and other spiritual creatures. Marlowe's Faustus is not simply a black magician out to sate his every desire, and neither is he an official doctor ensconced within the halls of legitimate Church institutions such as the university. Rather, in his use of the magic circle, he is someone who does not or cannot see the distinction between the natural and supernatural, the cosmic forces of Orion and the Antarctic and the spiritual forces of angels and demons.

Interestingly, the dramatic staging of this scene is almost entirely left out of Goethe's version of the Faust myth. But the motif of the circle persists throughout the early scenes of Goethe's text. In the first book of *Faust* (1808), Goethe has Faust ruminate for pages, in a melancholy state exemplary of the German-Romantic anti-hero, on his search for ultimate knowledge. Like Marlowe's Faustus, Goethe's Faust also abandons the official human knowledge of philosophy, science, and religion. For Faust, the world remains hidden, and it is doubtful that any *human* knowledge or access to the world will reveal anything of worth. Faust laments, "That I might see what secret force / Hides in the world and rules its course. / Envisage the creative blazes / Instead of ruminating in phrases."[27] Faust's impatience with book-learning leads him to a kind of Romantic embrace of the world in itself, though even in this gesture Faust takes with him a book of magic: "Flee! Out into the open land! / And this book full of mystery, / Written in Nostradamus' hand - / Is it not amble company?"[28]

While there is no magic circle scene like we see in Marlowe's version, Goethe does give us something like a magic circle, though all the drama takes place in its contemplation. In his search for ultimate knowledge, Faust is led to first contemplate the symbol of the macrocosm, perhaps of the type frequently encountered in Renaissance alchemical treatises – a spherical diagram showing the cosmos and all of its layers.

Again Goethe's Faust, like Marlowe's Faustus, notes the mystery of the hiddenness of the world. What divine force is it, Faust asks, that "Make nature's hidden powers around me, / manifest?"[29] This meditation prompts Faust to the epiphany of the interconnectedness of all things. As he notes, "Though every nerve, my veins are glowing." And again: "All weaves itself into the whole, / Each living in the other's soul."[30]

Yet, this first "dramatic" contemplation of the world's hiddenness only leaves Faust in despair. His only realization is the limit of all human knowledge. Picking up another book, Faust gazes upon a symbol of the earth spirit (*Erdgeist*), leading him to a second contemplation. Modern commentators have debated what exactly this earth spirit is – another name for an alchemical symbol, a pagan symbol linked to cyclic or seasonal time, or a Romantic personification of nature. Whatever it is, it prompts Faust, with some excitement, to ruminate on the elemental mysteries of the planet – Faust notes, in short, staccato phrases, the clouds, storm winds, the moon, and the sea. It finally leads Faust to actually evoke the earth spirit, which appears as a flame whose light is too bright for Faust to bear. Abstractions of the magic circle appear elsewhere in Goethe's *Faust* – a crowd of townspeople at a festival make a circle around Faust to commend him; at the same festival an anonymous black dog seems to follow and makes circles around Faust; later, in the conversation between Faust and Mephisto, the latter is blocked from leaving Faust's study due to a magical pentagram that has been placed above the door. These and other instances reinforce Goethe's abstraction of the magic circle, which comes to have the central characteristic brought forth in Faust's contemplations: the magic circle as that which paradoxically reveals the hiddenness of the world-in-itself.

2. Wheatley's *The Devil Rides Out* ~ Blish's *Black Easter, or Faust Aleph-Null*

Adaptations of the Faust myth in modernity are innumerable. While it is not my aim here to document each and every one of them, let us note just two 20th century examples, specifically for the way they take up the magic circle motif. Published in 1934, Dennis Wheatley's sensationalist novel *The Devil Rides Out* contains what is perhaps among the most detailed and elaborate magic circle scenes in the horror genre. The novel features, as its protagonist, the Duke de Richleau, a dashing and gentlemanly figure whose background in the dark arts helps him to solve mysteries that outwit even British Intelligence. Wheatley wrote several novels featuring Richleau, and in *The Devil Rides Out* a furtive black magician attempts to lure some of Richleau's friends into a coven of witches. In this, as other Wheatley novels, Richleau fights magic with magic, not unlike the van Helsing character in *Dracula*; it is therefore Richleau's intimate knowledge of the dark arts that makes him its greatest foe.

In the midst of an elaborate plot involving Satanism in modern London, Wheatley's novel has Richleau and his friends make a final stand against the black magician Mocata. In this scene, at the home of one of his friends, Richleau patiently makes preparations for the construction of a magic circle. After removing all furniture and rugs, the group – Richleau, Richard (an unswerving skeptic), Mary Lou, and Simon – proceeds to sweep and mop the floor. As Richleau comments, "I would like the room gone over thoroughly, since evil emanations can fasten on the least trace of dust to assist their materialization."[31] The group then changes into simple, freshly cleaned clothes. Taking a piece of chalk, string, and ruler, Richleau then proceeds to draw a perfect circle on the floor. To this outer circle he adds an inner circle. Then to this he draws a five-pointed star, whose points touch the outer circle and valleys touch the inner circle. Around the rim Richleau inscribes in Latin an exorcism text, along with ancient symbols, including Cabbalistic signs from the Sephiroth. Richleau then completes the "astral fortress" with a number of objects: silver cups with holy water, placed at the valley of the pentacle, long white candles at the apex of the pentacle, horse shoes, mandrake roots, and, for each person, rosaries, a string of garlic, asafetida grass, and phials of salt and mercury.

Richleau explains the rules of the game and what is at stake: "What may happen I have no idea...I cannot tell you what form his attack is likely to take...He may send the most terrible powers against us, but there is one thing above all others that I want you to remember. As long as we stay inside this pentacle we shall be safe, but if any of us sets one foot outside it we risk eternal damnation."[32] What does happen happens in phases. The first phase appears not to be supernatural at all, and involves psychological or affective disturbances (one of the characters, Richard, grows impatient when nothing happens, and is about to exit the circle to go to bed). A second phase involves anomalies of the room itself (unnatural play of light and cast shadows, violent winds in the room that come from nowhere). These merely pave the way for a third phase of strange "ab-human" creatures (a viscous dark shadow cumulating on the ceiling, then "a dim phosphorescent blob...shimmering and spreading into a great hummock...It had no eyes or face but from it there radiated a terrible malefic intelligence."[33]) The climactic moment comes when, all else failing, an angel of death in the form of a shadowy black stallion comes to claim their lives. Richleau must resort to a secret incantation (from the "Sigsand manuscript") that finally wards off this last attack. (The Hammer Studios 1968 adaptation of *The Devil Rides Out* spends a great deal of time on this scene, in which, interestingly, the magic circle becomes a kind of allegory for film in general and horror film in particular.)

At each stage of the attack Richleau and his friends are tested. Up until this point in the novel we have no real, direct evidence of the supernatural. Though we hear of a Satanic coven, and though Richleau, we are told, is in possession of erudite knowledge on the topic, we as readers never witness the supernatural in real time. Here, the magic circle drawn, the rules of the game established, and the play begun – here, the supernatural is able to manifest itself. First it comes in a form nearly indistinguishable from idealism (that is, from the *thought* of the supernatural, as possible or impossible). Then it comes in the form of inanimate, elemental forces (light and darkness, flame and shadow). This leads to its manifestation in the abject monster, the "nameless Thing" undulating and writhing just outside the circle's edge. Finally, the figure of death itself approaches, whose personification in the stallion masks the deeper metaphysical unknown of death itself. The magic circle is both what allows the "hiddenness" of the world to reveal itself, as well as that which protects the human subject from the rational unacceptability of this hidden, world-in-itself. It can be written off as mere illusion and trickery, an over-active imagination, and so on. But if, as Huizinga reminds us, the magic circle is also a mirror of the world, then the hiddenness of the world must also be understood as more than mere idealism, more than "it's all in your head"...

Wheatley's novel takes up the traditional notion of magic as presented in the Faust stories by Marlowe and Goethe. Here magic is not completely divorced from something called science, but neither is it simply equivalent to it. In these instances magic – and in particular black magic – is deemed an illegitimate form of knowledge primarily because it stands opposed to both the orthodox religious worldview (the world as divine creation) and the then-burgeoning scientific worldview (the world as knowable in itself through reason and experiment). The knowledge gained by black magic is neither the knowledge of the world as given to us by the divine Logos, nor is it the knowledge produced by the machinations of human reason. The knowledge of black magic is – or claims to be – a knowledge of the world as essentially hidden, rather than given (religion) or produced (science). The knowledge it lays claim to is, for this reason, occult knowledge, but knowledge that is only made apparent within the topography of the magic circle.

But while much of the dialogue in Marlowe and Goethe surround the status of human knowledge, we forget that the primary motive for Faust is practical – that is, the instrumentality of such occult knowledge. What happens when one takes occult knowledge not just as a philosophical problem, but as a resource to be harnessed and transformed into a tool? Certainly this happens to some extent in Wheatley's novel, where Richleau fights magic with magic, pitting occult knowledge against occult knowledge. But for all its evocative aesthetics of black magic, *The Devil Rides Out* remains firmly inscribed within a conventional moral framework (White Magic vs. Black Magic). What Richleau never talks about is the practical paradox of instrumentalizing the hidden world – that is, of taking that which by definition we as human beings cannot comprehend, and transforming it into a tool...or a weapon.

This is the theme of James Blish's novel *Black Easter*, which originally contained the subtitle *Faust Aleph-Null*. Published in 1968 as part of a larger series of works dealing with religion and science fiction, *Black Easter* takes up the Faust myth and places it in the modern context of nuclear war. The premise of the novel is straightforward – a wealthy arms manufacturer named Baines seeks to release all the demons on the world for a day. Presumably he, like Faust, has exhausted all the knowledge of his field, all the means of making weapons and accumulating global capital. The only weapon left undeveloped is in fact the supernatural one, the weapon of all weapons. In his search he contacts a reputed sorcerer named Theron Ware, who works as a sort of noir-esque private detective (much to the chagrin of the Church). Ware minces no words with Baines, stating with great sobriety, "All magic – I repeat, *all* magic, with no exceptions whatsoever – depends on the control of demons."[34] In Blish's near-future scenario, we get glimpses of a number of modern institutions, including the Consolidated Warfare Service, the Reformed Orthodox Agnostic Church, government think-tanks on weaponized anti-matter, a report titled *The Effects of Atomic Weapons*, and secret arms deals that feed directly into the ongoing Israel-Palestine conflict.

The climax of *Black Easter* is the actual evocation scene, depicted as something between Faust's conjuration and an experiment in particle physics. In a laboratory, Ware consults a panoply of grimoires, including the notorious *Grand Grimoire*, to ostensibly outdo Faust a hundredfold. "Ware stared at the Grand Circle for a moment, and then walked around it clockwise to the lectern and unlocked the book of pacts. The stiff pages bent reassuringly in his hands. Each leaf was headed by the character or sign of a demon; below, in special ink reserved for such high matters – gall, copperas, gum arabic – was the text of Theron Ware's agreement with that entity, signed at the bottom in his own blood, and by the character of the demon repeated in its own hand."[35] What follows in the novel is Ware's almost endless list of demons, their names, signs, and descriptions.

Of course this, like all such experiments, goes horribly wrong – or really, it goes too well. All the demons are loosed upon the Earth, followed promptly by natural disasters and the Emergency Broadcast System. In the panic, Baines, speaking to a military scientist, unrepentantly exclaims, "we're turning out to be wrong about the outcome – but no matter what it's *our* outcome. We contracted for it. Demons, saucers, fallout – what's the difference? Those are just signs in the equation, parameters we can fill any way that makes the most immediate sense to us. Are you happier with electrons than with demons?"[36] The cataclysm concludes with the arrival of Baphomet, who speaks, with great dramatic flair, as the voice of the cataclysm itself: "WE WILL DO WITHOUT THE ANTICHRIST. HE WAS NEVER NECESSARY. MEN HAVE ALWAYS LED THEMSELVES UNTO ME."[37]

On one level, *Black Easter* is easily understood as an allegory for the atomic age and the looming threat of Mutually Assured Destruction. We get black magic instead of atomic physics, sorcerers instead of scientists, warring nations instead of warring religions, and so on. But *Black Easter* is not a work of fantasy; arguably it isn't even a work of speculative fiction. The allegorical reading gives way, at a certain point, to a reading of the novel that is metaphysical. Taking the novel in this way does not mean, however, that one has to accept or reject the real existence of magic. The metaphysics of the novel lies in its evocation of the world and its hiddenness, especially when the hidden world is cataclysmically revealed through weapons that make it nearly impossible to distinguish a human-made war, a naturally occurring disaster, and a religious apocalypse.

3. Hodgson's *Carnacki the Ghost-Finder* ~ "The Borderland" (*Outer Limits*)

Up to this point we've been considering variations on a theme: that of cultural representations of the magic circle in its occult usage. In these stories the magic circle maintains a basic function, which is to govern the boundary between the natural and the supernatural, be it in terms of acting as a protective barrier, or in terms of evoking the supernatural from the safety inside the circle. We can now take another step, which is to consider instances in which the anomalies that occur are not inside or outside the magic circle, but are anomalies *of* the magic circle itself. This need not mean that the magic circle malfunctions, or has been improperly drawn. In some cases it may mean that the magic circle – as the boundary and mediation of the hidden world – itself reveals some new property or propensity.

A case in point is in the "occult detective" subgenre, a style of fiction popular in the 19th century. In these types of stories, a hero-protagonist combines knowledge of modern science with that of ancient magic to solve a series of crimes and mysteries that may or may not have supernatural causes. Algernon Blackwood's *John Silence – Physician Extraordinary* and Sheridan Le Fanu's *In a Glass Darkly* are examples in fiction, while Charles Fort's *The Book of the Damned* is an example in non-fiction. These types of stories are not only the precursors to modern-day TV shows such as *X-files* or *Fringe*, but they also bring together science and sorcery into a new relationship.

Published as a collection in 1913 as *Carnacki the Ghost-Finder*, William Hope Hodgson's occult detective stories are noteworthy for their reinvention of the magic circle. Hodgson's detective, named Thomas Carnacki, not only has at his disposal a deep and erudite knowledge of the occult, but he also has an array of gadgets, tools, and gizmos. Unlike many of the other occult detectives, who solve mysteries by crafty ratiocination, Carnacki combines rational "scientific" thinking with the appropriate tools for the job. Some of these tools are simple and low-tech, such as candle wax to seal windows and doors (thereby indicating if an entry was made during the night). Other tools are, by early 20th century standards, quite modern: Carnacki frequently makes use of photography in attempts to visualize spirits that may be invading a house or room. Still other tools are ancient and magical: Carnacki makes use of water circles and frequently refers to the Old English "Sigsand manuscript" for particular spells or incantations.

These types of tools are used mostly to document a presence that may or may not be supernatural. However the tool that trumps all the others is one of Carnacki's own design and invention: the "Electric Pentacle." It is featured in a number of the Carnacki stories. In "The Gateway of the Monster," Carnacki investigates the haunting of a particular room in a house. Residents complain of slamming doors, moving furniture, and strange, floating drapes. In itself the symptoms are unremarkable – your classic gothic haunting. But Carnacki's approach is unique. Determined to spend the night in the room (dubbed the "Grey Room"), Carnacki first draws a traditional magic circle on the floor, with the aid of the Sigsand manuscript. As with our previous examples, this serves as a barrier or protection against what Carnacki calls the "Outer Monstrosities."

But this in itself is not enough. Here Carnacki calls upon esoteric research, including a lecture by one Professor Garder, "Astral Vibrations Compared with Matero-involuted Vibrations below the Six-Billion Limit." Summarizing the research, Carnacki notes: "When they surrounded the Medium with a current, in vacuum, he lost his power – almost as if it cut him off from the Immaterial. That made me think a lot; and that is how I came to make the Electric Pentacle, which is a most marvelous 'defence' against certain manifestations."[38] Using vacuum tube technology, Carnacki in effect invents a steampunk magic circle:

"I turned now to fit the Electric Pentacle, setting it up so that each of its 'points' and 'vales' coincided exactly with the 'points' and 'vales' of the drawn pentagram upon the floor. Then I connected up the battery, and the next instant the pale blue glare from the intertwining vacuum tubes shone out."[39] While Marlowe and Goethe implicitly combine science and magic in their theories, here Hodgson materially combines them in the layering of the traditional pentacle with its vacuum tube, steampunk cousin.

In most of the cases the Electric Pentacle serves Carnacki well as a barrier, whether it is from a giant "death Hand," the eerie "blood drip," a "Saiitii manifestation," or the "Ab-human" shadows of the "Outer Worlds." In one case, however, the Electric Pentacle does something different. In the story "The Hog," Carnacki attempts to cure a man possessed by the images and sounds of a horde of cosmic pigs. Convinced that the man is not simply mad or hallucinating, he ensconces him within an elaborate version of the Electric Pentacle, with different colored vacuum tubes signaling different kinds of manifestations. Far from serving as a protective barrier, the center of the circle itself actually becomes a portal to another dimension, turning into a misty, bottomless, black pit: "A very curious thing happened then, for all around the edge of the pit, that looked so peculiarly like black glass, there came a sudden, luminous glowing...and, abruptly, out of the tremendous Deep, I was conscious of a dreadful quality or 'atmosphere' of monstrousness that was coming up out of the pit."[40] What finally emerges is a surreal, demonic animal: "I saw it pale and huge through the swaying, whirling funnel of cloud – a monstrous pallid snout rising out of that unknowable abyss...A pig's eye with a sort of hell-light of vile understanding in it."[41] In Hodgson's Carnacki stories, the Electric Pentacle is a hybrid of magic and science that, in stories like "The Hog" serves to invert the traditional uses of the magic circle. Instead of providing protection and serving as a barrier between the natural and supernatural, the Electric Pentacle actually focuses and intensifies the passage between them, whereby the "hidden world" reveals itself as a sort of extra-dimensional monstrosity.

This same idea is seen in "The Borderland," an episode of the classic TV series *Outer Limits*. Aired in 1960 and directed by Leslie Stevens, the episode also juxtaposes science and magic, though in ways different from the occult detective genre. The episode opens, significantly, with a séance. An old, wealthy industrialist is attempting to reach his son, who has recently died in a car accident. However, not all present are convinced of the spiritual medium, and one of the assistants calls their bluff, revealing a simple cloth-and-string rig. After the failure of the séance, a discussion ensues about the possibility of reaching the dead. The others present at the table are scientists, working on the use of modern turbine power to open a gateway to the fourth dimension. Using a simple demonstration of magnets and an introductory lecture in quantum physics, the scientists convince the industrialist to use the city's entire power plant for a brief period of time to try to open the gateway. The caveat is that whoever goes through to the other side must also search for the industrialist's dead son.

The bulk of the episode details the experiment. Unlike the Electric Pentacle, which in form and function remains a traditional magic circle, here the magic circle is different. In the center of the lab, a large chamber serves as the platform or portal. Around it is arranged various unnamed laboratory technology – huge magnets, electron scanners, and tape-driven computers. This "black box" is the magic circle, and its techniques are not magic but laboratory physics, its animating principle not the magical word or sign but the principle of atomic magnetism. The episode documents the experimental protocols for each phase of the experiment, as laboratory technicians recite in monotone voices instructions and data, sounding like a very different type of grimoire. At the experiment's peak, the scientist does enter into the fourth dimension, depicted in the episode as a wonderful montage worthy of Surrealist cinema. Space and time collapse in the consciousness of the scientist, but the search for the dead is for naught. If the occult detective genre still attempted to strike a balance between science and magic, *Outer Limits* episodes like these make a claim for bleeding-edge science as the new occultism, and electromagnetic laboratory chambers like the one we see as the new magic circles. If the lab is the circle, then the lab experiment is the magical ritual.

4. Lovecraft's "From Beyond" ~ Ito's *Uzumaki*

At this point we can pause for a brief review. In our previous *lectio*, the magic circle serves as a portal or gateway to the hiddenness of the world. In some cases the use of the circle actually guarantees the separation of the natural and supernatural, while also making possible the manifestation of the latter in the former. This is the case in the Faust stories by Marlowe and Goethe, where passages between nature and supernature are relatively restricted. While the supernatural is evoked, the division of natural and supernatural remains intact.

By the end of Marlowe's play, for instance, Faustus is dragged down to Hell, and the cosmology of the world remains as it has been.

But we've also seen that the ritual aspect of the magic circle has a wider impact, affecting anomalies in the weather, in everyday objects, in the beliefs and desires of individuals, and even – as in Goethe's *Faust II* – in the events of world history. The supernatural begins to bleed into the natural. The magic circle, whose function was to govern the boundary between them, begins to spiral out of control, as the human subjects "in" the magic circle struggle to control and comprehend that which lies outside of it (and thus outside the scope of human knowledge). Wheatley's *The Devil Rides Out* deals with these struggles on the level of religious morality, while Blish's *Black Easter* deals with them on the level of geopolitics and nuclear war. Gradually the boundary between the natural and the supernatural – topographically ensured by the use of the magic circle – is becoming more and more fuzzy. The final stage of this fuzziness is when the magic circle itself starts to behave anomalously, as we've seen in the occult detective subgenre. In some cases, the circle inverts its traditional function and amplifies the blurriness of the supernatural and the natural.

The *Outer Limits* episode ends on a note of caution, with humanity saving the world from its own inventions. But not all modern scientific incarnations of the magic circle are so filled with optimism. We get a slightly different, more menacing picture from early 20th century writers in the "weird fiction" tradition like H.P. Lovecraft. Lovecraft's short story "From Beyond," published in 1934 in the pulp magazine *Fantasy Fan*, takes the technological magic circle in a different direction. Instead of serving as a gateway or portal to other dimensions – a function still very much within the traditional magic circle – Lovecraft's characters construct a magic circle whose function is the dissolving of the boundary between the natural and supernatural, the four-dimensional and the other-dimensional, the world revealed and the world as hidden. This dissolving of boundaries between the natural and supernatural is also found in the work of contemporary authors influenced by Lovecraft, including Caitlín Kiernan, Thomas Ligotti, China Miéville, and filmmakers such as E. Elias Merhige. In Lovecraft's story, what results is a "subtractive" magic circle, which by its very receding into the background bizarrely flattens all dimensions into one.

In "From Beyond," the narrator recounts the experiments of one Crawford Tillinghast, a reclusive physicist who begins to explain his rationale as follows: "We see things only as we are constructed to see them, and can gain no idea of their absolute nature. With five feeble senses we pretend to comprehend the boundlessly complex cosmos, yet other beings with a wider, stronger, or different range of senses might not only see very differently the things we see, but might see and study whole worlds of matter, energy, and life which lie close at hand yet can never be detected with the senses we have."[42] Tillinghast continues, a little excitedly, announcing "I have always believed that such strange, inaccessible worlds exist at our very elbows, *and now I believe I have found a way to break down the barriers*" (in Lovecraft's inimitable prose, italics always indicate an epiphany of cosmic horror...).[43] Tillinghast goes on to show the narrator a device he has constructed, set up in the center of the laboratory, which Lovecraft only describes as a "detestable electrical machine, glowing with a sickly, sinister, violet luminosity."[44]

Seated around the device, in the center of the lab, the narrator and Tillinghast re-enact the magic circle of Faustus and his later incarnations. When Tillinghast turns on the device, the narrator experiences an influx of color and shape. Quickly, however, the trip begins to turn sour: "At another time I felt huge animate things brushing past me and occasionally *walking or drifting through by supposedly solid body*."[45] Finally, the narrator "sees" around him that which has always existed but which

boundary or point of mediation between two different ontological orders, two different planes of reality. Lovecraft discards the architectonics of the magic circle, but keeps the metaphysics. The device serves as nothing more than a nodal point from which the characters are able to "see" the extra-dimensional reality and the weird creatures that swim about them every day. The aim, then, of the device as a magic circle is primarily a philosophical one: rather than assuming the division between the natural and supernatural, and then utilizing the magic circle to manage or govern the boundary between them, in "From Beyond" the magic circle is used to reveal the already-existing non-separation between natural and supernatural, the "here and now" and the "beyond."

A third and final transformation to the magic circle has to do with *the disappearance of the circle itself*, while its powers still remain in effect. During the story, as the characters witness the "beyond," the device itself gradually recedes into the background as the characters can only look about in a state of horrified awe. It is as if we get the effects of the magic circle, but without the magic circle itself. Nearly all the traditional uses of the magic circle adopt the model of spectator and spectacle – inside the circle is the audience, and outside it is the dramatic action (again, this is most explicit in the film version of *The Devil Rides Out*). In "From Beyond," however, we lose this separation, and there is no spectacle that we may view from inside the safety of the circle. Instead, natural and supernatural blend into a kind of ambient, atmospheric no-place, with the characters bathed in the alien ether of unknowable dimensions. The center of the circle is, then, really everywhere...and its circumference, really nowhere.

This third transformation – in which the magic circle as such is diffused into the world – is the principle motif in Junji Ito's manga series *Uzumaki*. First appearing in Shogakukan's *Weekly Big Comic Spirits* in the 1990s, Ito's manga tells the story of a small Japanese town that is mysteriously afflicted by the symbol of the spiral. The spiral first appears as the obsession of several townspeople, one of whom – a Mr. Saito – begins to see spirals everywhere – in a snail's shell, in the swirling river water, in incense smoke, in hand-made pottery, in tapestry designs, even in the fish cakes in his udon soup. As he frantically comments to a friend, "...I find the spiral to be very mystical...It fills me with a deep fascination...like nothing else in nature...no other shape."[49] In a final, desperate attempt to achieve this mystical union with the spiral, Saito's body itself undergoes a spiral-metamorphosis. His eyes swirl around in opposite directions (so he can see the whole world as a spiral...), his tongue twists inward like a spiral, and his entire body twists and curls itself into a giant, fleshy spiral.

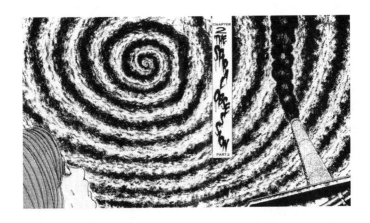

Not only does the "spiral obsession" become contagious, affecting people throughout the town, but, more importantly, the spiral begins to manifest itself in strange and unnatural ways: at the cremation of Saito, the ashes and smoke rise into the sky, forming a menacing, dark spiral shape with vague hints of ghostly faces floating within it. In the scenes that follow, the townspeople discover spiral-shaped grass growing in the hills, spiral-shaped clouds in the sky, spiral-shaped mud and clay from the town river, and so on.

Thus what begins as a psychological and subjective *obsession* quickly turns into an objective *manifestation* in the world. In one episode, a potter discovers that the clay he uses seems to be imbued with unnatural capacities, forming grotesque, spiral-like forms, with hints of horrific, haunting faces deep within the clay itself. In nature (the river, the sky, the mud), in the body (the eyes, tongue, ears, hair), and in art (ceramics and clay pottery; tapestry design), the spiral manifests itself both in and as the world.

Uzumaki adds yet another dimension to the magic circle motif we've been tracing. The spiral is, in one sense, an abstract, geometrical shape. It has no actual existence in the world, except as a manifestation in the form of a spiral (a snail's shell, a slice of fish cake). This paradoxical state means that the spiral can only be said to negatively exist – the spiral in itself is never manifest except as a spiral "in" some thing, in the world. This sort of bleed-over effect of the abstract into the concrete world is different from our traditional examples of the magic circle. In Goethe's *Faust*, we saw that Faust only encounters the magic circle symbolically, in his contemplation of the abstract symbol of the macrocosmos. But the abstract symbol and the concrete manifestation remain separate; Faust' contemplation of the symbol in itself does not lead to the evocation of demons or magic. In *Uzumaki*, by contrast, something else happens in the relationship between the abstract and the concrete, between symbol and manifestation. On the one hand, the spiral has no existence except as manifestation – and it is this contagious, pervasive manifestation that the characters describe as unnatural or strange. On the other hand, throughout the *Uzumaki* series, the spiral is more than just a pattern in nature – it is also equivalent to the *idea* of the spiral itself. That is, the abstract symbol and the concrete manifestation are inseparable, to the point that the outer world of the spiral's manifestation can "infect" or spread into the ideational world of the spiral as an idea. Beyond a geometrical symbol, and beyond a pattern in nature, the spiral in *Uzumaki* is ultimately equivalent to thought itself – but "thought" understood here as not simply being the interior, private thoughts of an individual. Instead, the spiral-as-thought is also "thought" as unhuman, "thought" as equivalent to the world-without-us. In this sense *Uzumaki* suggests that the Absolute is horrific, in part because it is utterly unhuman.

In the examples of Lovecraft's "From Beyond" and Ito's *Uzumaki* we see that the traditional magic circle is no longer needed in order to think about the hidden world. This is because, as the stories imply, we are already bathed in the invisible viscous hiddenness of the world. In a kind of perversion of Kantian philosophy, Lovecraft and Ito suggest that the world-in-itself is only "hidden" to the extent that our phenomenal experience of the world is determinatively a human one. In fact, Lovecraft and Ito implicitly make the argument that not only is there no distinction between the natural and supernatural, but that what we sloppily call "supernatural" is simply another kind of nature, but one that lies beyond human comprehension – not in a relative but in an absolute sense. Herein lies the basis of what Lovecraft called "cosmic horror" – the paradoxical realization of the world's hiddenness as an absolute hiddenness. It is a sentiment frequently expressed in Lovecraft's many letters: "Now all my tales are based on the fundamental premise that common human laws and interests are emotions have no validity or significance in the vast cosmos-at-large. To me there is nothing but puerility in a tale in which the human form – and the local human passions and conditions and standards – are depicted as native to other worlds or other universes. To achieve the essence of real externality, whether of time or space or dimension, one must forget that such things as organic life, good and evil, love and hate, and all such local attributes of a negligible and temporary race called mankind, have any existence at all...but when we cross the line to the boundless and hideous unknown – the shadow-haunted *Outside* – we must remember to leave our humanity and terrestrialism at the threshold."[50]

In our readings of the magic circle and the hidden world, Lovecraft's "From Beyond" and Ito's *Uzumaki* act as a hinge, between the more traditional uses of the magic circle (which maintain the relation between the revealed world-for-us and the hidden world-in-itself), and a different, more unconventional variant of the magic circle. That unconventional type of magic circle is one in which the metaphysical principle remains in effect, but the magic circle itself disappears. It is a kind of non-human, anonymous "magic" without any "circle" to inscribe it. What would this mean? For one, it implies that any magic without a circle is also a magic without human agents to cause, control, or utilize magic. But what would magic without the human mean? What would it mean to have revealed to us the hiddenness of the world without any human to evoke that revelation?

Excursus on Mists and Ooze

In "From Beyond" Lovecraft's characters are suspended in a strange no-place that is neither the normative, human world of scientific laws and therapeutic religion, nor is it the purely supernatural domain of the heavens or the underworld. Once the device is turned on, they cease to be in the magic circle per se, as it is impossible to distinguish the world outside from the world inside the circle. They seem to almost swim about in a thick, viscous ether of unknown dimensions. In Ito's *Uzumaki* the magic circle as a symbol diffuses into the world itself, to the point that it infects both the natural world and the very thoughts of the characters. This strange disappearing act of the circle already gives us a clue to our earlier question of magic without the circle. In particular, what is revealed in such instances is not just the world understood scientifically. What is revealed is a world that is neither quite natural nor supernatural, not quite the normal "here and now" and not quite the unknowable "beyond." Perhaps, instead of a magic *circle*, we have something like a magic *site*.

The magic site is, simply, the place where the hiddenness of the world presents itself in its paradoxical way (revealing itself – as hidden). In some cases magic sites are like magic circles, constructed by human beings for specific purposes. This is the case with the mad scientist theme in the Lovecraft story. More often than not, however, the magic site spontaneously happens without any human intervention. The magic site need not be on sacred ground, and it need not have special buildings or temples constructed for it. It can be in the darkest, most obscure, hidden caverns or underground fissures. It may be an accidental or unintentional site – the site of an archaeological dig, the site of a mining operation, the site of a forest or underground subway tunnel. Whereas the magic circle involves an active human governance of the boundary between the apparent world and the hidden world, the magic site is its dark inverse: the anonymous, unhuman intrusion of the hidden world into the apparent world, the enigmatic manifesting of the world-without-us into the world-for-us, the intrusion of the Planet into the World. If the magic circle is the human looking out and confronting the unhuman, anonymous, hidden world, then the magic site is that hidden world looking back at us. It is not surprising, then, that whereas the magic circle evokes vaguely anthropoid creatures (demons, ghosts, the dead), the magic site creeps forth with entities that are neither animate nor inanimate, neither organic nor inorganic, neither material nor ideal.

Let us introduce a new terminology to talk about the ways in which the magic site – as opposed to the magic circle – creeps forth. The magic site manifests the hidden world revealed in two forms: as *mists* and *ooze*. Mists evoke many things – drizzling rain, a dense fog, or surreal clouds in the overcast sky. Natural formations like clouds or rain are, certainly, entities inscribed within the scientific study of atmospheric conditions. But the term "mists" may also refer to any inanimate entity that lies somewhere between the air and the ground. For instance, nephology, the scientific study of clouds, considers clouds not only on the Earth but on any planet where conditions are conducive to cloud formation – indeed in interstellar space, where gravity fields may attract cosmic dust into nebulae. The ethereal nature of mists means that while they may appear solid and to have distinct forms, they are also immaterial, and can readily become formless.

The same applies to ooze. Again, the term "ooze" evokes more that which oozes than a discrete, static thing. What oozes can be slime, mud, oil, or pus. Ooze can ooze on the body, in the ground, in the sea or space. Slime, for instance, can be understood in a scientific scene (for instance in plant microbiology or prokaryotic biology), but slime is also something between a liquid and a solid. Ooze may also be metamorphic and shape-shifting, as with the organisms classed as *myxomycota*, which, during their life cycle, may alternately behave like plants, fungi, or amoeboid organisms. Despite their differences, mists and ooze are two examples of the ways in which the "hidden" world reveals itself, and often with strange and weird effects.

Mists and ooze populate many of our speculative fantasies about the end of the world. In our fifth *lectio* let us consider, briefly, a few examples of cataclysmic mists in the genres of science fiction and horror, before going on to a consideration of ooze in our sixth and final *lectio*.

5. Shiel's *The Purple Cloud* ~ Hoyle's *The Black Cloud* ~ Ballard's *The Wind From Nowhere*

There are, of course, a number of modern novels and films that portray mists as gothic, malevolent forces, often that serve as cover for ghosts, monsters, or unknown miasmas. Novels such as James Herbert's *The Fog* (1975) and Stephen King's *The Mist* (1980), as well as John Carpenter's film *The Fog* (1980) all fall into this category. The mist in these types of stories is not only itself vaguely material and formless, but in many cases its origin and aims remain utterly unknown to the human beings that are its victims. Arguably, the text that establishes the blueprint for this type of story is M.P. Shiel's 1901 novel *The Purple Cloud*. Hailed by the likes of Lovecraft as a masterpiece of weird fiction, *The Purple Cloud* is a surreal and sometimes wandering narrative about a mysterious purple gas that emerges from the North Pole and spreads over the entire planet, killing every living being in its path - except for one person, whose recently-discovered journal of the aftermath of the purple cloud constitutes the novel itself.

Shiel's novel borrows from the "last man" motif popularized by works such as Mary Shelley's underrated *The Last Man* (1826). But whereas most last man stories depict a definable cause for the extinction of humanity (war, plague, a comet), Shiel's novel abstracts the cataclysm into a roving, amorphous mist, whose origin is described in surreal, unhuman terms by the last surviving human being: "The lake, I think, would be something like a mile wide, and in its middle is a pillar of ice, low and thick; and I had the impression, or dream, or fantasy, that there is a name inscribed round in the ice of the pillar in characters that could never be read; and under the name a lengthy date; and the liquid of the lake seemed to me to be wheeling with a shivering ecstasy, splashing and fluttering, round the pillar, from west to east, with the planet's spin; and it was borne in upon me – can't say how – that this fluid was the substance of a living being..."[51] Here we have the magic site from which the mist emerges, flowing deep within the undiscovered coldness of the North Pole. Approaching this site, the narrator experiences something like a dark ecstasy, verging on delirium – a "most cold, most mighty high – had its hand of ice on my soul, I being alone in this place, face to face with the Ineffable; but still, with a gibbering levity, and a fatal joy, and a blind hilarity, on I sped, I span."[52]

In *The Purple Cloud* we see a mist emerge from within the Earth, a mist that menacingly washes over the surface of the planet, described by Shiel in an almost eschatological manner. A variant on this theme comes from a novel by the astrophysicist Fred Hoyle – *The Black Cloud*. Published in 1957 as a pulp SF novel, *The Black Cloud* involves a mysterious body of black mass that appears to be heading straight for Earth. A group of American astrophysicists are the first to detect the interstellar anomaly through their high-tech telescopes: "If you look carefully at what seem like very big clouds, you'll find them to be built up of lots of much smaller clouds. This thing you've got here seems, on the other hand, to be just one single spherical cloud."[53] Rational observation and pragmatic urgency are the order of discourse in this novel. At an international meeting convened to discuss the pending danger, one scientist notes, "I find that if the results that have been presented to us this afternoon are correct, I say if they are correct, then a hitherto unknown body must exist in the vicinity of the solar system. And the mass of this unknown body must be comparable with or even greater than the mass of Jupiter itself."[54] As the black cloud approaches, it starts to become visible to the naked eye, and general panic sets in – there are eyewitness reports of a "general blackness in the sky," a "yawning circular pit," and newspaper reports of a "celestial black-out." As it comes nearer to Earth, atmospheric and biospheric changes rapidly occur – global temperatures drastically increase, there are warm rains in Iceland, an exponential increase in insect speciation in the southern hemisphere, and "the deserts flowered as they had never done at any time while Man had walked the Earth."[55]

Hoyle's treatment of the hidden world theme is markedly

different from that of Shiel. While both novels involve a mist that threatens to destroy the planet and render humanity extinct, Shiel's treatment is much more rooted in the tradition of apocalyptic mysticism. Shiel's prose descriptions read more like one of William Blake's prophecies than as science fiction, and by the novel's end this tendency is reinforced even more. By contrast, Hoyle's narrative is much more in line with Cold War-era "hard" science fiction. Scientists from all disciplines convene to study, hypothesize, and develop an action plan for the black cloud. While the character of Shiel's novel comes to relate to the hidden world in terms of mysticism and destiny, the characters in Hoyle's novel have no time for existential angst, as they are caught up in the production of knowledge and the preparations for an impending disaster. In Shiel's novel the end actually does come – or at least one version of the end. In Hoyle's novel, by contrast, the end is narrowly averted (a *deus ex machina* frequently used in 19th century "comet" stories of the same type). Finally, in *The Purple Cloud* the magic site – the site from which the mist manifests itself – is that of the Earth itself, a literally encircled whirlpool of animate gas. In *The Black Cloud*, however, the mist comes from outer space, suggesting that the hidden world is also a hidden cosmos.

The presence of a magic site – some locale from which the hidden world can manifest itself, often with disastrous effects – implies some point of origin for the hidden world, or at least for its manner of manifesting itself to us as human beings. In *The Purple Cloud* and *The Black Cloud* it is through mist that the hiddenness of the world manifests itself, though their magic sites differ (the cold heart of the Earth in one, and the depths of interstellar space in the other). What happens when this strange, cataclysmic mist is present, but without a point of origin? This is the idea behind J.G. Ballard's first novel, *The Wind From Nowhere*. Published in 1961, the novel has become something of a cult classic, ironically due to Ballard's repeated attempts to disown it throughout his life. Taking place in modern London – as well as at different locales across the globe – *The Wind From Nowhere* begins with your run-of-the-mill hurricane, which proceeds to turn into a worldwide cyclone that makes the Earth all but uninhabitable for human beings. In its episodic format, we see a range of human individuals coping with the wind, and the dense storms of dust and dirt that accompany it: "The wind had reached 250 mph and the organized resistance left was more interested in securing the minimal survival necessities – food, warmth, and 50 feet of concrete overhead – than in finding out what the rest of the world was doing, knowing full well that everywhere people were doing exactly the same thing. Civilization was hiding. The earth itself was being stripped to its seams, almost literally – six feet of topsoil were now traveling through the air."[56]

"It's hard to describe," one character says, a "solid roaring wall of black air – except that it's not air any more but a horizontal avalanche of dust and rock."[57] Eventually the realization sets in – the wind may continue to increase in velocity until the planet becomes almost completely composed of winds and gases. As one scientist notes, "we're witnessing a meteorological phenomenon of unprecedented magnitude, a global cyclone accelerating at a uniform rate, exhibiting all the signs distinguishing highly stable aerodynamic systems."[58] (It also contains a number of rather awkward jabs at humor, like the following exclamation by one character, during one of the wind storms in southern Europe: "So much of life in the States – and over here for that matter – could use a strong breath of fresh air."[59]) By the novel's end the wind abates without warning or cause, just as mysteriously as it had begun. But throughout the novel, Ballard traces a theme that would become common in many of his novels – the correlation between internal states and external states, between the inner turbulence of modern, alienated subjectivity, and the outer turbulence of an equally

unspecified menace that threatens a Cold War-era town and its inhabitants. *The Blob* relies on a fairly conventional relationship of inside and outside, "us" and "them," with the key to survival laying in the protection of the former from the invasion of the latter.

But not all ooze-horror stories utilize this inside-outside boundary. That the gooey entity in *The Blob* comes from outer space – the outside of all outsides, as it were – is noteworthy, for it implies a safe boundary that must be secured at all costs. Other ooze-horror films depict the entity coming not from outside but from inside, from within the Earth itself. This is exactly what happens in the 1959 Italian film *Caltiki the Immortal Monster*. Directed by Riccardo Freda and Mario Bava – two directors who reinvented the Italian horror film – *Caltiki* is in many ways a classic, low-budget, monster movie. Shot in black and white, with stilted acting and special effects techniques that include a giant honey-drenched cheesecloth, *Caltiki* takes the ooze-horror motif in a different direction that of *The Blob*.

In *Caltiki* the ooze comes not from outer space, but from the bowels of the Earth. The oozing creatures are linked to an ancient Mayan myth about an indescribable monster – Caltiki – raised by vengeful gods. The film itself takes place in modern Mexico, where we find an American team of government scientists conducting an archaeological dig. Amid the all-too-human drama of lover's quarrels and tensions between the local villagers and the American scientists, the expedition comes across an ancient, underground temple – that also happens to contain buried treasures, and a very high degree of radioactivity. This is the magic site, a forgotten, dead temple that contains a still living curse. Once Caltiki is revived – as the expedition attempts to steal away the relics and treasures – it proceeds to attach itself to anything and everything in sight. Eating away the flesh of any living thing, Caltiki stumbles, like a giant, drunken, undulating amoeba, into the nearby town. In the lab, scientists examine a piece of Caltiki that has broken off; their studies suggest that Caltiki is a giant unicellular organism over 20 million years old. Meanwhile, in scenes both wonderful and abject, Caltiki proceeds to engulf houses, cars, animals, and people, able to grow and divide itself in the process. The scientists finally crack and mystery and discover that only fire can kill Caltiki, at which time a battalion of tanks with flamethrowers comes to the rescue. The ancient curse is again put to rest...for the time being.

In *Caltiki* we see ooze depicted allegorically, either as the revenge of nature (the Earth "biting back" against its colonizing intruders), or as the revenge of culture (ancient Mexico biting back against American pillaging). But at some point in the film's action, these allegorical readings recede into the background, and what comes to the fore is the strange, faceless, formlessness of the ooze itself. It seems to have no motive, no vendetta, no program of action, other than simply that of "being ooze." This anonymity is matched by the affective sliminess of Caltiki, as if it in itself were literally the bowels of the Earth. Thus, whereas films like *The Blob* imagine threats *to* the world coming from outside, a film like *Caltiki the Immortal Monster* turns this around and imagines a threat that *is* the world, coming from within.

Another variation on this theme comes from the 1956 British film *X: the Unknown*. Whereas *Caltiki* gives us the example of ancient ooze, *X: the Unknown* gives us the example of modern, industrial ooze. In both films the magic site lies buried under the Earth. But whereas the magic site in *Caltiki* is a buried temple, in *X: the Unknown* the magic site is a radioactive field previously used for weapons testing. Presumably too many bombs have inadvertently created a fissure in the ground, out of which "Monster X" emerges, with a ravenous appetite for any source of electrical energy. A group of British military men and an American scientist attempt to study Monster X. Similar to Caltiki, Monster X is also an oozing, formless mass that resembles mud more than slime. At one point the scientist gives a mini-lecture on geology, suggesting that Monster X was originally a primordial form of life buried in the Earth's depths, which has adapted itself to feed off of energy (including radioactive energy). But the scientist, lacking a solution for stopping Monster X, wonders to himself: "but how do you kill mud?" In a moment of irony not uncommon in monster movies, the characters realize that to defend itself against the ooze, humanity must in effect destroy the Earth.

Both *Caltiki* and *X: the Unknown* feature monsters that frustrate the traditional inside/outside boundary established by films like *The Blob*. They both feature a magic site, deep within the crusts and caverns of the planet, in which the hidden world oozes and gropes forth to the surface, threatening the human beings that inhabit this surface. This surface/depth boundary is slightly different for each film, however. In *Caltiki* the depth is archaeological, in that it references ancient, lost civilizations; here the magic site itself was also once a magic circle. In *X: the Unknown* the depth is geological, in that the animate, radioactive mud that oozes to the surface is itself inseparable from the sedimentary layers from which it comes; here the magic site, while enabled by human actions (e.g. weapons testing), remains utterly unhuman.

In our consideration of ooze – as one facet of the hidden world – we have one more step to take, and that is to consider ooze not only as archaeological and geological, but noological as well. Here ooze is not just a biological amoeba, and not just the mud of the Earth; here ooze begins to take on the qualities of thought itself. Consider Fritz Leiber's short story "The Black Gondolier," published in the 1964 Arkham House anthology, *Over the Edge*. In this story, the narrator recounts the events that led to the mysterious disappearance of his friend Daloway, a recluse and autodidact living nearby oil fields in southern California. Daloway, it seems, began to develop a bizarre and unnatural fascination with oil – not just as a natural resource, and not just as something of geopolitical value, but with oil in itself as an ancient and enigmatic manifestation of the hidden world. Over time Daloway's conversations with the narrator begin to take on the form of mystical visions. Oil, he notes, constitutes "that black and nefarious essence of all life that had ever been…a great deep-digged black graveyard of the ultimate eldritch past with blackest ghosts."[60] As a kind of gothic, funeral ooze, Daloway tries to convince the narrator that "oil had waited for hundreds of millions of years, dreaming its black dreams, sluggishly pulsing beneath Earth's stony skin, quivering in lightless pools roofed with marsh gas and in top-filled rocky tanks and coursing through a myriad channels…"[61]

The image of oil as stealthily waiting gives the ooze the vague quality of intelligence and intent – and, more specifically, of malefic intent. In Leiber's hyperbolic prose, oil is not the type of ooze that we see in *Caltiki* or *X: the Unknown*, where the ooze remains hidden beneath the surface of the Earth. Instead, in "The Black Gondolier" oil is described as an animate, creeping ooze that already is on the surface, and that immanently courses through all the channels of modern industrial civilization, from the central pipelines feeding the major cities to the individual homes and cars that populate those cities. At one point in the story, the narrator attempts to put Daloway's crackpot theories into coherent form: "Daloway's theory, based on his wide readings in world history, geology, and the occult, was that crude oil – petroleum – was more than figuratively the life-blood of industry and the modern world and modern lightening-war, that it truly had a dim life and will of its own, an inorganic consciousness or sub-consciousness, that we were all its puppets or creatures, and that its chemical mind had guided and even enforced the development of modern technological civilization."[62] "In brief," the narrator notes, "Daloway's theory was that man hadn't discovered oil, but that oil had found man."[63]

While the oil in "The Black Gondolier" is, like the monsters in *Caltiki* and *X: the Unknown*, an instance of the hidden world manifesting itself as ooze, there are some striking differences between them as well. For instance, the monsters in *Caltiki* and *X: the Unknown* are anomalies of nature (effected by radiation or mining), whereas the oil in "The Black Gondolier" is sentient and malefic precisely because it is natural to the planet. The oil is not so much a product of human design or intervention, as we have in the other examples, but the reverse – it is human "modern technological civilization" that is the effect, the product of this sentient, creeping oil. In addition, both *Caltiki* and *X: the Unknown* rely on the governance of boundary relationships – *Caltiki* inverts the inside/outside relationship of *The Blob*, while *X: the Unknown* shifts things to a surface/depth relationship. In "The Black Gondolier" we see yet another shift, and that is to a relationship of continuity/discontinuity. The monsters in *The Blob*, *Caltiki*, and *X: the Unknown* remain, even though they are formless monsters, discrete entities. They creep, crawl, and undulate forward. One can point to them, isolate them, and even firebomb them. Thus their formlessness – their "ooziness" – is still constrained by the outline of their form. In "The Black Gondolier" any attempt to point to or isolate oil in total is futile, precisely because it is fully continuous, not only with the Earth, but also with modern industrial society. (I write this during the tragic saga of the Gulf oil spill, the scale of which eerily evokes Leiber's story, as well as Reza Negarestani's inimitable *Cyclonopedia*.)

Arguably, this image of sentient ooze effects a further transformation of the "hidden world" theme that we've been tracing. The final scenes of the story, in which Daloway is silently carried into a great undulating "sea" of oil in the middle of the night, asserts the decidedly unhuman and unfamiliar qualities of the ooze. Both of these presuppositions rely on a basic dichotomy between self and world, between the thinking subject (where thought is interiorized) and a non-thinking object (upon which thought is projected). All of this breaks down in the case of ooze. Oil does not simply become a "big brain," as if to recuperate all thought within the ambit of human thought. The oil in "The Black Gondolier" is both crude, material stuff, and immanent, miasmatic thought, both materially viscous and sentient. What we are presented with in "The Black Gondolier" is the suggestion that thought has always been unhuman.

Addendum: On Schmitt's *Political Theology*

The hiddenness of the world, whether revealed via the human-oriented motif of the magic circle, or the unhuman motif of the magic site, puts forth the greatest challenge, which is how to live in and as part of such hiddenness. In that ambivalent moment in which the world-in-itself presents itself to us, but without immediately becoming the human-centric world-for-us, might there be a way of understanding hiddenness as intrinsic to the human as well?

One of the insights of Carl Schmitt's 1922 book *Politische Theologie* (*Political Theology*) is that the very possibility of imagining or re-imagining the political is dependent upon a view of the world as revealed, as knowable, and as accessible to us as human beings living in a human world. As Schmitt notes, "all significant concepts of the modern theory of the state are secularized theological concepts not only because of their historical development – in which they were transferred from theology to the theory of the state, whereby, for example, the omnipotent God became the omnipotent lawgiver – but also because of their systematic structure..."[64] Such an analogy has an impact, Schmitt argues, for an understanding of the development of key political concepts, such as sovereignty and the state of exception. The most concise statement of the book comes a few lines later: "The exception in jurisprudence is analogous to the miracle in theology."[65]

But the way in which that analogy is manifest may change over time. Schmitt notes that the 17th and 18th centuries were dominated by the theological analogy of the transcendence of God in relation to the world, which correlates to the political idea of the transcendence of the sovereign ruler in relation to the state. By contrast, in the 19th century a shift occurs towards the theological notion of immanence (specifically, in modern pantheism and organicist philosophy), which likewise corre- lates to "the democratic thesis of the identity of the ruler and the ruled."[66] In these and other instances, we see theological concepts being mobilized in political concepts, forming a kind of direct, tabular comparison between cosmology and politics (God and sovereign ruler; the cosmos and the state; transcen- dence and absolutism; immanence and democracy).

Given this, what would it mean to consider a political theology of the hiddenness of the world (that is, an occult political theology)? To do so, we would have to avoid taking Schmitt's theory literally. This would not only recuperate the hiddenness of the world into the human frame, but it would also lead to rather absurd political models (in which, for instance, the hiddenness of the world would serve as an analogy for a similarly hidden form of governance, or the secret society as a political platform...). This is clearly not the direction one would want to take this idea. But where then?

Schmitt's analysis remains within the scope of the analogical framework, and the big question that comes out of *Political Theology* has to do with how decisions are reached as to the correlation of this or that world-view with this or that political system. However, what Schmitt pays less attention to is the way in which *the analogy itself* may come under question. As Schmitt himself notes, "the metaphysical image that a definite epoch forges of the world has the same structure as what the world immediately understands to be appropriate as a form of political organization."[67] The analogical framework presumes a few key things: First, that there is an accessible, revealed, and ordered world "out there" that may serve as a model or guide for the development of a political system "in here." This is, arguably, the basis of political philosophy itself. Second, it presumes that this analogical relation is a one-way street, in that the discernable order of the world flows directly into the constitution of politics, when clearly there are a number of ways in which the direction is reversed (as when politics determines how and whether we intervene in "the environment"). Finally, Schmitt's analogical framework is decidedly anthropocentric, taking for granted that politics – not unlike theology – deals first and foremost with the human (here the Hobbesian analogy of the body politic is the most explicit example of this kind of anthropomorphic quality of the political).

The question is, what happens when we as human beings confront a world that is radically unhuman, impersonal, and even indifferent to the human? What happens to the concept of politics once one confronts the possibility that the world only reveals its hiddenness, in spite of the attempts to render it as a world-for-us, either via theology (sovereign God, sovereign king) or via science (the organismic analogy of the state)? In the face of politics, this unresponsiveness of the world is a condition for which, arguably, we do not yet have a language. While the *lectio* above have focused on the cultural and philosophical ramifications of this situation, one has only to take a few steps to then consider what the hiddenness of the world might mean for thinking about the political.

Clearly there are no easy answers here. The "hiddenness of the world" is another name for the supernatural, exterior to its assimilation by either science or religion – that is, exterior to the world-for-us. But these days we like to think that we are much too cynical, much too smart to buy into this – the supernatural no longer exists, is no longer possible...or at least not in the same way. In a sense, it is hard to escape the sense of living in a world that is not just a human world, but also a planet, a globe, a climate, an infosphere, an atmosphere, a weather pattern...a rift, a tectonic shift, a storm, a cataclysm. If the supernatural in a conventional sense is no longer possible, what remains after the "death of God" is an occulted, hidden world. Philosophically speaking, the enigma we face is how to confront this world, without immediately presuming that it is identical to the world-for-us (the world of science *and* religion), and without simply disparaging it as an irretrievable and inaccessible world-in-itself.

III. Nine *Disputatio* on the Horror of Theology

In Medieval Scholasticism, disagreements or confusions on a given topic were often vetted through the *disputatio,* or disputation. Sometimes the *disputatio* would be tightly regulated, as when two scholars would debate an agreed-upon topic. But on other occasions the *disputatio* could be about any topic, about "whatever" – in this case they would be referred to as *disputatio de quodlibet.* Such intellectual free-for-alls were often quite spontaneous and associative. These "whatever" *disputatio* could also be written down, in which the author would engage in a *disputatio* with him or herself. It is in this spirit that the following essays-in-miniature are presented. Each deals with the way that supernatural horror mediates between life and death, often by evoking some concept of "life-in-itself" that hovers between the domains of science and religion, biology and theology – it is in this in-betweenness that one discovers supernatural horror as a way of thinking about life beyond either the subjective (life-experience) or the objective (life science) definitions.

The question that runs through these *disputatio* is the following: What if "horror" has less to do with a fear of death, and more to do with the dread of life? Not a very uplifting thought, that. Nevertheless, death is simply the non-existence after my life, in a sense akin to the non-existence before my life. These two types of non-existence (*a parte post* or after my life, and *a parte ante* or before my life) are mirrors of each other. This is a sentiment repeatedly voiced by Schopenhauer: "For the infinity *a parte post* without me cannot be any more fearful than the infinite *a parte ante* without me, since the two are not distinguished by anything except the intervention of an ephemeral life-dream."[68]

If horror – as we've been discussing it – is a way of thinking the world as unthinkable, and the limits of our place within that world, then really the specter that haunts horror is not death but instead life. But what is "life"? Perhaps no other concept has so preoccupied philosophy, with such divergent opinions on what is or isn't the essence of life. After thousands of years of philosophical inquiry, we can be pretty sure that we will never arrive at a definitive and final answer to the "what is life" question. And yet life, as lived, constantly throws the question back at us – the most immediate is the least understood. In addition, "life" is not really a philosophical concept. Philosophers talk endlessly about metaphysical concepts such as "being," "substance," or "existence," whereas "life" seems to slip by the wayside, not quite a primary metaphysical concept, and yet more than its scientific or religious definitions. In fact, "life" is interesting for philosophy precisely because of the way it seems to be nestled between its scientific and religious definitions, both of which steer life towards human life, the life-for-us.

So the question really is: Can there be a philosophy of "life" that does not immediately become a concern of either Being or God? To what extent is "life" as a concept always situated between a non-ontological "life itself" (the view of science) and an onto-theology of the life-beyond-the-living, or afterlife (the view of religion)?

1. After-Life

Ever since Aristotle distinguished the living from the non-living in terms of *psukhē* (ψυχη) – commonly translated as "soul" or "life-principle" – the concept of life has itself been defined by a duplicity – at once self-evident and yet opaque, capable of categorization and capable of further mystification. This duplicity is related to another one, namely, that there are also two sides to Aristotle – there is Aristotle-the-metaphysician, rationalizing *psukhē*, form, and causality, and there is Aristotle-the-biologist, observing natural processes of "generation and corruption" and ordering the "parts of animals."

Despite the voluminous output of Aristotle's natural philosophy of life, there is relatively little about death – or, for that matter, the afterlife. But what comes "after life"? Is it death, decay, and decomposition, or is it resurrection and regeneration? Is it, in biological terms, the transformation of the living into the non-living, from the organic life of molecules to non-organic matter? Or does it involve a theological re-vitalization of the resurrected, living cadaver? In either case, the after-life bears some relation to the "during life" and the "before life," and it is precisely the ambiguity of these relationships that has shaped the debates on mechanism and vitalism in the philosophy of biology, as well as the earlier debates in Scholasticism on the nature of creaturely life.

There is no better guide to the after-life than Dante. The life of the after-life in the *Commedia* is a political theology, at once rigidly structured and yet coursing with masses of bodies, limbs, fluids, fires, rivers, minerals, and geometric patterns of beatific light. In particular, the *Inferno* gives us several concise statements concerning the life of the after-life. In the seventh circle, Dante and his guide Virgil come to the "burning desert," upon which a multitude of bodies are strewn about.[69] Among them Dante and Virgil come across Capaneus, one of the seven kings who assaulted Thebes and defied the law of Jove. Capaneus lies stretched out on the burning sand, a rain of fire descending upon him, while he continues his curses against the sovereign. As Virgil explains, Capaneus is one of the blasphemers, grouped with the usurers and sodomites for their crimes against God, State, and Nature, respectively. But, as with many of Dante's depictions in the *Inferno*, there is no redemption, and the punished are often far from being penitential. Their tired, Promethean drama of revolt, defiance, and blasphemy goes on for eternity.

It is easy to read such scenes in a highly anthropomorphic

manner. But each individual "shade" that Dante encounters is also associated with a group or ensemble that denotes a category of transgression, and this is especially the case of Middle Hell. Upon entering the gates of the City of Dis, Dante and Virgil are first confronted by a horde of demons, and then by the Furies. Once they are able to pass, they come upon a "landscape of open graves," each one burning and holding within it one of the Heretics. The scene is depicted with great drama by Gustave Doré, who, following the prior example of Botticelli, presents the heretics as a mass of twisted, emaciated corpses emerging from their graves. Along the way they also encounter a river of bodies immersed in boiling blood (watched over by a regiment of Centaurs), as well as the "wood of suicides," in which the bodies of the damned are fused with dead trees (watched over by the Harpies). Within many of the circles, Dante encounters nothing but multiplicity – bustling crowds (the Vestibule of the Indecisive), a cyclone of impassioned bodies (Circle II, the Lustful), a sea of bodies devouring each other (Circle V, the Wrathful), dismembered bodies (Circle VIII, the Sowers of Discord), and a field of bodies ridden with leprosy (Circle VIII, the Falsifiers). The life-after-life is not only a life of multiplicity, but it is also a life in which the very concept of life continually negates itself, a kind of vitalistic *life-negation* that results in the living dead "citizens" of the City of Dis.

Perhaps, then, one should begin not by thinking about any essence or principle of life, but by thinking about a certain negation of life, a kind of life-after-life in which the "after" is not temporal or sequential, but liminal.

2. Blasphemous Life
But we've forgotten about blasphemy. What is blasphemy in regard to the forms of life-negation found in the *Inferno*? Returning to the burning desert, Capaneus, noticing Dante's inquiring gaze, shouts back to him: "What I was once, alive, I

still am, dead!"[70] On one level this is simply a descriptive statement – defiant towards divine sovereignty in life, I remain so in the after-life. But surely Capaneus realizes that, after life, resistance is futile?[71] Or have the terms changed, after life? Perhaps his words do not mean "I am still defiant" but rather, quite literally, something like "I am a living contradiction." Such phrases denoting a living death recur in the *Inferno*, often spoken by Dante himself.[72] Perhaps, then, this phrase "What I was once, alive, I am still now" actually means – in the afterlife – that "I am still living, even in death." This living contradiction – being *living dead* – is also linked to the political-theological contradiction of a power that at once "shuts down" as much as it "lets flow." There is a kind of Medieval biopolitics in the *Inferno* quite different from the modern, Foucauldian version. The strange conjunction of sovereignty and multiplicity in the *Inferno* does not demand the punishment of souls, but instead requires a mass of animated, sensate, living bodies, in some cases resulting in an almost medical concept of the after-life (e.g. the Sowers of Discord are meticulously dismembered, dissected, and anatomized). In tandem with a sovereign "shutting-down" we have also a kind of governmental "letting-flow"; indeed, at several points the *Inferno* seems to imply their isomorphism.

Blasphemy, then, can be viewed in this regard as the assertion of living contradiction. But this assertion is not simply a resistance to an authoritative demand to be non-contradictory. In its modern variants it strives to become an ontological principle as well. Nowhere is this more evident than in the "weird biologies" of H.P. Lovecraft's *At the Mountains of Madness*.[73] The narrative describes two kinds of blasphemous life. The first involves the discovery of unknown fossils and a "Cyclopean city" in the deep Antarctic, both of which display "monstrous perversions of geometrical laws."[74] The discovery leads to the remains of an unrecognizable, intelligent species of "Old Ones" that, in the Lovecraftian mythos, are thought to have lived eons prior to the earliest known human fossilized data.[75]

But this only leads to a further revelation, in which the explorers discover another type of life which they call the Shoggoths, and which seem to resemble formless yet geometric patterns: "viscous agglutinations of bubbling cells – rubbery fifteen-foot spheroids infinitely plastic and ductile – slaves of suggestion, builders of cities – more and more sullen, more and more intelligent, more and more amphibious, more and more imitative..."[76] In Lovecraft's prose, the Shoggoths are the alterity of alterity, the species-of-no-species, the biological empty set. When they are discovered to still be alive, they are described sometimes as formless, black ooze, and sometimes as mathematical patterns of organic "dots," and sometimes as a hurling mass of viscous eyes. Formless, abstract, faceless. In an oft-referenced passage, what the narrator expresses is the horizon of the ability of the human characters to think this kind of "life":

> ...when Danforth and I saw the freshly glistening and reflectively iridescent black slime which clung thickly to those headless bodies and stank obscenely with that new unknown odor whose cause only a diseased fancy could envisage – clung to those bodies and sparkled less voluminously on a smooth part of the accursedly resculptured wall in a series of grouped dots – we understood the quality of *cosmic fear* to its uttermost heights.[77]

What Lovecraft puts forth in his tales of cosmic horror is a form of blasphemy that is decidedly non-anthropomorphic and misanthropic. At the mountains of madness we move from a concept of blasphemy as grounded in human agency (the blasphemy of Capaneus in the underworld) to a blasphemy of the unhuman ("more and more amphibious"). For Lovecraft, "it" is blasphemous – but also indifferent, incomprehensible, and in many cases unnamable ("the thing," "the doom," "the fear," "the whisperer").

At the center of blasphemous life is this idea of the living contradiction. *Blasphemous life is the life that is living but that should not be living.* This contradiction is not a contradiction in terms of medical science; the blasphemous life can often be scientifically explained and yet remain utterly incomprehensible. If it is a logical contradiction, it would have to be one in which the existence of true contradictions would not only be admitted, but would be foundational to any ontology. In logical terms, the assertion that there are true contradictions is often referred to as "dialetheism."[78] But with Lovecraft we have a twist. The Shoggoths are bizarre examples of *dialethic biologies*, contradictions that are living precisely because they are contradictory, or "blasphemous."

Whereas for Dante the blasphemous is the living contradiction – to be living in death, to be living after life – for Lovecraft the blasphemous is the very inability to think "life" at all. Blasphemy is here rendered as the unthinkable. To account for such blasphemous life, one would have to either compromise existing categories of thought, or entertain contradictory notions such as "living numbers" or "pathological life."

3. Ambient Plague

The anonymous "it" of blasphemy is also expressed in the hermeneutics of plague and pestilence. Our very concepts regarding disasters generally betray a profound anxiety. That some disasters are "natural" while others are not implies a hypothetical line between the disaster that can be prevented (and thus controlled), and the disaster that cannot. The case of infectious diseases is similar, except that the agency or the activity of this "biological disaster" courses through human beings themselves – within bodies, between bodies, and through the networks of global transit and exchange that form bodies politic. In the U.S., the two-fold conceptual apparatus of "emerging infectious diseases" (naturally-caused) and "biodefense" (artificially-caused) cloaks a generalized militarization of public health. More fundamentally, when it becomes increasingly more difficult to discern the epidemic from the bioweapon, entire relations of enmity are redefined. The threat is not simply an enemy nation or terrorist group, the threat is itself biological; biological life itself becomes the absolute enemy. Life is weaponized against Life, resulting in an ambient *Angst* towards the biological domain itself.[79]

However, while it has become customary to view epidemics in light of post-germ theory, "autoimmunitary" boundary disputes, there is a more fundamental problem articulated in the pre-modern concept of plague and pestilence, where biology and theology are always intertwined in the concepts of contagion, corruption, and pollution.[80] One of the central concerns of chroniclers of the Black Death was that of causality, and how causality was interpreted in relation to the divine.[81] As the Black Death spread throughout Medieval Europe, the motif of the "angry God" recurs in many of the chronicles, both fictional and non-fictional. It forms of key framing-tool for Boccaccio's *Decameron*, is a motif in *Piers Plowman*, and it shapes the sub-genre of plague pamphlets in England.[82] These in turn make reference to the examples of Biblical plague, of which the most well known is the Ten Plagues of Egypt, in which God sends down ten "plagues" to persuade the Egyptian pharaoh to free the Jewish people.[83] Here the "plagues" do include epidemic disease, but also rivers that turn into blood, swarms of insects, tempestual storms, and an eclipse. Another, more common reference among the Black Death chronicles is apocalyptic. *Revelations*, with its dense and complex symbology, tells of "Seven Angels" sent forth to deliver "Seven Plagues" that are to be "poured" upon mankind as a form of divine judgment; here again the "plagues" range from contagious disease to aberrations in livestock, the weather, and the destruction of human cities.[84]

In all these instances we see this key element: a divine sovereign who, in the form of a judgment and/or punishment, sends down – or better, emanates – a form of miasmatic life that is indissociable from decay, decomposition, and death. What is noteworthy about the pre-modern concept of plague and pestilence is not only its blurring of biology and theology, but the profound lability that the concepts of plague and pestilence have. In the chronicles of the Black Death, plague seems to be at once a separate, quasi-vitalized "thing" and yet something that spreads in the air, in a person's breath, on their clothes and belongings, even in the glances between people. As one early chronicler notes, "one infected man could carry the poison to others, and infect people and places with the disease by look alone."[85]

It is tempting to understand the Medieval hermeneutics of plague and pestilence as Neoplatonic – a supernatural force emanating from a divine center. However this would require that we understand the relation between Creator and creatures as pathological, a divine sovereign that emanates itself through a miasmatic diffusion of decay. But what is being emanated here is not creation itself but rather its opposite, a kind of de-creation that occupies the underside of what Aristotle called "passing away" (disease, decay, decomposition).[86] This strange type of life, that seems to emanate from a Neoplatonic One and diffuse itself throughout creaturely life, cannot be understood without taking into account another element. As varied as the Medieval accounts of plague and pestilence are, one of the common motifs, along with the angry God, is that of plague and pestilence as a divine weapon. The divine sovereign doesn't simply pass judgment; the sovereign weaponizes life – the pathological life of "plagues" – and turns it against the earthly life of the creature, itself a product of the divine will.

Arguably this motif has its roots in antiquity: in Hesiod, for instance, we see how Zeus sends the "gift" of plague-ridden Pandora to Prometheus as a form of retribution; likewise *The Illiad* opens with an angry Apollo sending down "arrows" of plague upon the armies of men for their disrespect towards the gods. There are earthly instances of this as well. An oft-mentioned example in this regard is the Medieval practice of catapulting corpses. The primal scene in this regard is the 14th century Italian trading post at Caffa, on the northern border of the Black Sea. Ongoing skirmishes between Italian merchants and Muslim locals led, in one instance, to the catapulting of plague-ridden corpses by the latter, over the fortress walls of the former.[87]

All of this is to suggest that the political theology of pestilence is not an issue of shutting-down or "walling." It is, certainly, that, but only to an extent. For the pervasive, diffuse, and circulatory quality of pestilence – this "thing" or "event" that is at once a divine emanation and yet a source of social and political chaos – raises a more complex problem for sovereign power: how to control the pervasiveness of pestilence without losing control of the pervasiveness of people.

But it is not clear in the accounts of chroniclers, or in the texts of Boccaccio, Chaucer, or Langland, if pestilence is that which causes social and political disorder, or if pestilence is identical with this affective fantasy of total chaos. So we have a strange situation in which pestilence, itself supernaturally caused by a divine, primary sovereign power, then elicits a host of exceptional measures by a secondary, earth-bound sovereign, in order to ward off the pending and pervasive chaos that pestilence occasions – which itself emanates from the primary, divine sovereignty – the *primum mobile* of pestilence, as it were.

4. *Nekros*

However, it should not be forgotten that the weaponized plague always targets a body or bodies. And what, indeed, is the target of the living weapon, if not the living target – that is, the corpse?

The concept of *nekros* (νεκρος) has two significant meanings in classical culture. On the one hand, *nekros* is the corpse or the dead body. In the *Odyssey*, for instance, when Odysseus organizes the funeral rites for one of his companions, it is the *nekros* that is burned at the grave site: "Once we'd burned the dead man (*nekros*) and the dead man's armor,/heaping his grave-mound, hauling a stone that coped it well,/we planted his balanced oar aloft to crown his tomb."[88] Certainly *nekros* names the singularity of the departed life, or of life recently departed from the body, leaving behind a corpse. But this corpse retains something residual of that life, insofar as both the corpse and its armor are together set upon the grave. We might even say that *nekros* not only names the "dead man," but also the thingness of the corpse. In a sense *nekros* oscillates between the body-minus-life and the thingness of the corpse, the latter approaching the domain of the purely non-living (e.g., the armor as the non-living body).

However the *Odyssey* also contains another, more significant usage of *nekros*. This comes in the well-known passages recounting Odysseus' journey to the underworld. In this scene Odysseus first performs a sacrificial rite that calls to the dead, who then emerge from the underworld in a kind of slow-motion swarming:

> And once my vows
> and prayers had invoked the nations of the dead (*ethnea
> nekrōn*),
> I took the victims, over the trench I cut their throats
> and the dark blood flowed in – and up out of Erebus they
> came,
> flocking toward me now, the ghosts of the dead and gone
> (*nekuōn kataethnēōtōn*)[89]

Here *nekros* no longer names the corpse, nor even the thingness of the corpse. Instead, *nekros* names something alive, or at least vitalized – but in a way fundamentally different from the life of animals. *Nekros* as the corpse presumes a reliable boundary between life and death, whereas *nekros* as "the dead" are characterized by an ambivalent vitalism. These dead souls are immaterial and yet not transcendent, a life that at once continues to live on but that lives on in a kind of interminable, vacuous, immortality. *Nekros* is thus not the corpse but rather "the dead," or the existence of a life-after-life.

But what, if anything, "lives on" after life? Paul provides one example, which would become a center of dispute in later theological debates over resurrection. The mortal body, like all living things, displays both an infusion of life-spirit as well as processes of growth. "But God gives it a body as he has determined, and to each kind of seed he gives its own body...So also is the resurrection of the dead. The body that is sown is perishable, it is raised imperishable...It is sown a natural body: it is raised a spiritual body."[90] The organicist motif of resurrection is that of a seed that is sown in the earth and that grows and is animated (or re-animated) into a new body, the latter being both the resurrection of the person as well as that of the community of the *corpus mysticum*.

There is also a great deal of ambiguity in the Pauline formula. Patristic thinkers differed on what kind of life-after-life resurrection was, and how such a supernatural form of life was to take place.[91] One set of debates centers around the problem of the temporality of resurrection. If the living, mortal, earthbound body was susceptible to the processes of growth and decay, then in what material state would the body be resurrected? What kind of life returns? Would the resurrected body – the life-after-life – live in a state of perpetual stasis (as a kind of "living statue"), or does it still undergo transformations, either in the form of higher perfections, or in terms of a beatific hypergrowth? The so-called material continuity debates among Patristic thinkers not only highlights the problem of time in relation to life and after-life, but it points to a problem that cuts across the theological and political domains (for instance, when Paul lays out the basic anatomy of the *corpus mysticum* as constituted both by the natural and supernatural, earthly and divine).

Resurrection could be resurrection of the body, the soul, or more generally of "the dead." But even theories of the resurrection of the soul – as one finds in Origen's notion of a "spiritual body" – still maintain the minimal necessity of a body-in-flux. The problems of material continuity are also linked to spatial and topological problems concerning the material process by which the formless body of decay and putrefaction is re-assembled and re-vitalized. The mere return of material particles does not constitute resurrection, for those particles must be ensouled, renewed, or in some way cast anew. And here the almost absurdist debates concerning "chain consumption" come into the foreground. If the corpse is devoured by worms and beasts, and those beasts are in turn devoured by man, how can the parts or particles of the body be re-assembled for resurrection? (One can imagine a solution to this problem offered by Alfred Jarry's King Ubu...) One partial resolution, offered by Tertullian, was to shift emphasis from the matter to the form of the resurrected body, so that continuity could exist through change. Cannibalism thus does not negate continuity, and thus the living dead can also be the eaten dead.

The theological debates over resurrection point to some basic dichotomies: should the organicist model of the growth and decay of the natural world (seeds, plants, animals) serve as the analogical model for resurrection, or are those processes precisely what resurrection aims to correct and to "heal"? Such questions have to do, in effect, with the nature and the supernature of the after-life, or better, with the relation between life and a "life-plus-something" that constitutes early Medieval theology and later Scholastic onto-theology. Insofar as the after-life is related in some way – as analogy, as model, as perfection – to finite, mortal life, it obtains a certain familiarity that enables thinkers such as Origen to talk at length about growth and decay in a theological context. But insofar as the after-life is a supernatural phenomenon, it remains outside the scope of philosophical and even theological inquiry.

How can life – something that is presumably *lived* – be situated at such a point of inaccessibility? In his classic 1917 text *Das Heilige* (*On the Holy*), theologian Rudolph Otto examines religious experience in a broad, global context, through his concept of the "numinous." The numinous is the limit-experience of the human confronting the world as absolutely non-human, the world as "wholly other," a "mystery inexpressible and above all creatures."[92] For Otto, the numinous describes a contradictory experience of horror and wonder that is encapsulated in his phrase, *mysterium tremendum*. Both mystery and the "overpoweringness" of tremors or terror play into Otto's theory of religious experience. "The truly 'mysterious object' is beyond our apprehension and comprehension, not only because our knowledge has certain irremovable limits, but because in it we come upon something inherently 'wholly other,' whose kind and character are incommensurable with our own, and before which we therefore recoil in a wonder that strikes us chill and numb."[93] While such events may indeed result in dramatic, intense experiences (such as that of mystics), they may also creep up on one in the most everyday or banal circumstances.

As Otto notes, this confrontation with the unhuman world may manifest itself as the various demons, ghosts, and malefic creatures that populate the mythological and cosmological framework of different religious traditions. We might also add that this confrontation with the divine as horrific is also a leading theme in the 18th century gothic novel. In gothic fictions, the numinous is ephemeral; it can either be revealed to have natural and rational causes (as in Radcliffe's *The Mysteries of Udolpho*), or the supernatural can be affirmed, and its horror sublimated into an affirmation of faith (Walpole's *The Castle of Otranto*), or a descent into damnation (Lewis's *The Monk*).[94]

The word "numinous" is etymologically akin to the Kantian term *noumena*. Kant's own re-affirmation of the split between *phenomena* (the world as it appears to the subject) and *noumena* (the inaccessible world-in-itself) tended to draw his analyses towards the former and away from the latter. Indeed, there is a sense in which Kant's antinomies of pure reason – the proofs for God's existence, the origin of the universe, and the existence of the soul – are pushed so far away from *phenomena* that they begin to occupy a space not that far from *noumena*.[95] And yet it is precisely this domain – the anonymous "there is" – that has for so long remained a point of attraction for ontology.

Let us consider a conceptual portmanteau, between the gothic "numinous" (the horror of the divine as absolute otherness) and Kantian *noumena* (the unhuman, anonymous world). In what sense is the *nekros* as "the dead," also a kind of *nouminous life*? A nouminous life would have to articulate a conceptual space that is neither that which is lived outside of discourse (the gothic "numinous"), nor that which is reasoned within discourse and yet unlived (the Kantian antinomies). We could call this a "horror of life" if such a phrase did not bring with it unwanted anthropomorphic and even existentialist connotations. Perhaps we can say that, if the life-after-life is a nouminous life, it is because it elicits a noumenal horror that is the horror of a life that indifferently lives on.

5. The Spirit of Biology
The relationship between theology and horror in the West invites a number of superficial comparisons: in the Eucharist there is both cannibalism and vampirism; in the Jewish and

Christian apocalyptic traditions the realization of the City of God always entails resurrection of the dead; and in numerous instances the New Testament portrays the demons and demonic possessions that elicit the healing powers of the Messiah. Indeed, considering the extent to which genre horror deals with the themes of death, resurrection, and the divine and demonic, one could argue that genre horror is a secular, cultural expression of theological concerns.

If we look more closely, however, we see that in many instances it is a concept of "life" that mediates between theology and horror. We can even imagine our theologians carefully watching the classics of 20th century horror film: the relation between the natural and the supernatural (Aquinas watching *The Cabinet of Dr. Caligari*); the distinction or non-distinction between human and beast (Augustine watching *The Wolf Man* or *Cat People*); the coherence or incoherence of the *corpus mysticum* (Paul watching *Revolt of the Zombies* or *I Bury the Living*); the problem of the afterlife (Dante watching the Italian silent film *L'Inferno*). But one need not imagine such scenarios, for many art-horror films deal with such issues, from David Cronenberg's early "tissue horror" films, to Ingmar Bergman's *Through a Glass Darkly*, to Dario Argento's now-complete "Three Mothers" trilogy.

If both theology and horror deal with the concept of "life," then what exactly is this "life" that lies at the limits of the thinkable? Aristotle gives us one clue. In the *De Anima* Aristotle explicitly thinks the question of life as a philosophical question, though the concept of *psukhē*: "It must be the case then that soul (*psukhē*) is substance as the form of a natural body which potentially has life, and since this substance is actuality, soul will be the actuality of such a body."[96] There is, to borrow terms that Scholasticism would favor, an "ensoulment" or animation that takes place in hylomorphism, a process through which life is literally formed (or in-formed…and sometimes de-formed).

However Aristotle gives us a slightly different picture in *De Generatione et Corruptione*. Here the central question is not about the principle of life, but rather about the problem of morphology and change. Aristotle asks, how are "coming-to-be" and "passing-away" different from change in general? Are growth and decay merely examples of the larger genre of change in itself? This in turn leads to a more fundamental question regarding the domain of the living: "What is 'that which grows'?"[97]

Aristotle's approach is to distinguish between different modalities of change. There are, first, the processes of alteration, which are qualitative (one thinks of a tree sprouting branches or an animal growing fur – the tree or animal remains the same kind of tree or animal). There are also the processes of coming-to-be and passing-away, which are substantial changes (as when one animal is eaten by another animal, the former undergoing modification in substance). Finally, there are the processes of growth and decay, which can involve changes in magnitude (growing larger or smaller). Now, while the first two are general processes of change that occur in the living and non-living, Aristotle implies that growth and decay are exclusive to the domain of the living. Why is this? One of the reasons Aristotle provides has to do with eating. Growth and decay, though exclusive to the living, fundamentally have to do with changes across the substance of the living and non-living, changes that may be due to "the accession of something, which is called 'food' and is said to be 'contrary' to flesh," and that involves the "transformation of this food into the same form as that of flesh."[98]

To Aristotle's example of nutrition we might also include the processes of decay and decomposition, the passage of *nekros* into non-living matter. Food for worms... But might we include another passage, that of *nekros* into the life-after-life? What sort of change would this be – alteration, coming-to-be/passing-away, or growth/decay? Would this constitute a kind of biology of spiritual transformation, or would it constitute the "spirit of biology"?

What theology implicitly admits, horror explicitly states: a profound fissure at the heart of the concept of "life." Life is at once this or that particular instance of the living, but also that which is common to each and every instance of the living. Let us say that the former is *the living*, while the latter is *Life* (capital L). If the living are particular manifestations of Life (or that-which-is-living), then Life in itself is never simply this or that instance of the living, but something like a principle of life (or that-by-which-the-living-is-living). This fissure between Life and the living is basically Aristotelian in origin, but the fissure only becomes apparent in particular instances – we see it in the Scholastic attempt to conceptualize "spiritual creatures," we see it in the problem of the life-after-life of resurrection, and we also see it in natural philosophy and the attempts to account for teratological anomalies and aberrations.

However, the most instructive examples come from classical horror film, in particular the "creature features" of Hollywood film studios such as Universal or RKO. The proliferation of living contradictions in horror film constitutes our modern bestiary. Let us consider a hagiography of life in the relation between theology and horror: the living dead, the undead, the demon, and the phantasm. In each case, there is an exemplary figure, an allegorical mode, a mode of manifestation, and a metaphysical principle that is the link between philosophy and horror.

With the living dead the exemplary figure is of course the zombie. Its allegorical mode has changed over time, but it is most often that of the uprising of the underclasses (the working class, the mob, and the masses are all represented in Romero's films). The zombie can manifest itself in many ways, as multitude (Romero's *Land of the Dead*) or as contagion (Fulci's *Zombie*). With the living dead, the guiding metaphysical principle is "flesh."

By contrast, the undead has its exemplary figure in the vampire. Its allegory is not with the rising of underclasses, but with a decaying, romantic aristocracy (evident quite early, in Stoker's novel). The vampire manifests itself in either human-animal metamorphoses (bats, rats, dogs), or in metamorphoses between the organic and inorganic (mists, smoke). While such metamorphoses indicate a near-immortality and an infinite changeability, the vampire is also haunted by mortality – sometimes as threat, sometimes as promise. The vampire's metaphysical principle is "blood."

The demon is an amalgam (partially material, partially immaterial) whose exemplary figure is itself an amalgam – that of demonic possession, and its strange and unnerving hybrid of human body and demon soul. The allegory of the demon is often middle class and bourgeois, sometimes within a therapeutic or even clinical framework (as evident in Renaissance narratives of possession or in modern films like *The Exorcist*). Being in the middle, as it were, the demon brings together the highest and the lowest, transforming the human into a beast, and the beast into a god. The demon's metaphysical principle is "meat."

Finally there is the phantasm, whose exemplary figure is the ghost. Whereas the three previous figures dealt with allegorical modes that reflected class dynamics (zombie-working class, vampire-aristocratic, demon-bourgeois), the ghost deals with that strange and unknown provenance after life – the domain of spirit, soul, or, in its secular sense, of memory. Despite their immateriality, ghosts also manifest themselves in various ways, either by spiritual mediums, by changes to objects in the physical world, or by signs and portents. The ghost's metaphysical principle is "spirit."

Generalizations such as these obviously have their limitations. But one thing to note is that in each case we have a form of life that at once repudiates "life itself" for some form of after-life. Each of these figures are literally living contradictions. The zombie is the animated corpse, the vampire is the decay of immortality, the demon is at once a supernatural being and a lowly beast, and the phantasm exists through materializations of its immateriality. And, in each case, the form of after-life works towards a concept of life that is itself constituted by a privation or a negation, a "life-minus-something"; the basic Aristotelian (and Hippocratic) concepts of flesh, blood, meat, and spirit are paradoxically living but without life. In this sense, *horror expresses the logic of incommensurability between Life and the living.*

6. Univocal Creatures

One of the peculiarities of Aristotle's *De Anima* is that, while it opens with the stated aim of inquiring into the "principle of life," it quickly by-passes this aim in favor of detailed analyses of the natural world, the senses, and the intellect. What ostensibly begins with an investigation into the bodies of living organisms (*zoē*) ends with a rather opaque meditation on thought (*nous*). It is almost as if Aristotle discovers that the question of "life" can only be ontological if it ceases to be a question of life-as-such. This has also colored later glosses on the text, such as those by Averröes and Aquinas, whose commentaries are characterized by this shift.

In Book II, however, Aristotle makes some important distinctions. After having offered the concept of *psukhē* as the life-principle, Aristotle distinguishes between different types of *psukhē* – that is, that *psukhē* is itself manifested in a range of specific forms. Aristotle distinguishes between plants, animals, and humans, based on the manifestation of *psukhē* or the life-form that governs them. While plants are characterized by a nutritive *psukhē*, animals are characterized by a sensory and motile *psukhē*, and humans by a reasoning or intellective *psukhē*. This forms an ascending order, for whereas plants are governed by nutrition, they can neither move nor think. The same follows for animals, lacking reason.

The Aristotelian framework was, of course, surpassed by the growth of natural history and, later, the emergence of a separate field of biology. But while the modern life sciences have analyzed the domain of the living down to the smallest molecule, the Aristotelian concept of a "life principle" remains contested terrain.[99] In particular, one issue left unresolved in the *De Anima* has to do with the concept of *psukhē* itself – the Life that is common to every instance of the living. Is there one, univocal *psukhē* that cuts across different domains of the living? Does *psukhē* in effect emanate from its ideal center towards the multitude of individual life forms? Or is there a *psukhē* that is proper to each individual, constituting a kind of propriety to *psukhē*?

Before Aristotle's "biological" works make their appearance in the twelfth century via Arabic translations, there were already attempts to indirectly think Life as a name of the divine. The creature, emblematic of the domain of the living, is always a symptom. It is an effect, a product – as Bonaventure would put it, a *vestigium* or "footprint" of the divine. The world of the living is a manifestation of a great *liber creaturae*, the "book of creatures." Life is precisely that which is symptomatic of the divine, though it is not of the divine itself.

But it is Aquinas who both synthesizes the various positions on the creature and emphasizes that the concept of the creature revolves around the relation between Creator and creature, supernatural and natural, light and mud. In his attempts to wed Aristotelianism with Christian doctrine, Aquinas offers a neat summary of what we might call the "creaturely triad." What is the relation between the creature and Creator, between the living and the divine Life that makes the living possible? Aquinas first sets up a dichotomy between two approaches, that of equivocity and that of univocity. In the first, there is no relation between creature and Creator, and the divine remains forever outside the possibility of being thought. In the second – univocity – there is a relation of continuity between creature and Creator, such that, in extreme cases, the latter can be said to be co-existent with the former. The problems with each, from Aquinas' position, are easy to see. While equivocity forecloses any possibility of thinking or experiencing the divine, univocity makes it too easy, in effect flattening the divine onto nature. As is well known, the solution offered by Aquinas is that of analogy. Between no relation (equivocity) and pure relation (univocity), there is partial relation, or analogy. Thus the creature is analogous to the Creator, their difference articulated in the form of degrees of perfection ("proportion" and "proportionality"). The creature is the life that is less-than-divine, the Creator is the life that is more-than-the-living.

Might we also then say that, for Aquinas, the living are analogously related to Life? Aristotle's question of "life" and the life-principle cannot be asked of Life as such. It can only be asked of the living, of something "beyond" the living or that forms the living. But then we would have to consider "life" in general as a kind of negative concept, a concept that at once asserts its asking as it recedes into the background of this question.

This negative concept of life is ontologized along two axes. The first is predicated on ontological difference. It posits a distinction, as we noted previously, between "Life" and "the living." The *De Anima* posits *psukhē* as a general life-principle, but at the same time distinguishes it from particular instances of the living in plant, animal, and human life. Everything hinges on the relation between Life and the living. In the period of high Scholasticism, the spectrum of creation, from monotheism to pantheism, from orthodoxy to heresy, illustrates the way in which the question of Life is never far from the question of the nature of the divine. In this sense the *De Anima* is ontologically prior to texts such as *De Partibus Animalium* and *Historia*

Animalium.

The non-concept of life is also aligned on a second axis, on which it is predicated on a distinction between a "principle of life" and its corresponding "boundaries of articulation" (this is its essence and existence, substance and accident). The principle of life may vary quite widely, from *psukhē* to a theological soul, to modern mechanism or "vital spirit," to contemporary concepts of molecule, gene, and information. But it always makes possible one or more boundary relations that, when applied to the domain of the living, re-affirm the principle of life as essence. Such boundaries include, first and foremost, that between the living and the non-living. Secondary ones include the division between the organic and inorganic, and between human and animal.

7. Extinction and Existence

The individual life can die. But what of "life" in general? This is the question posed by the disaster, for while any given disaster – natural or human-made – may not render all of life extinct, the disaster always contains in itself the threatening thought of extinction. "The disaster," writes Maurice Blanchot, "ruins everything, all the while leaving everything intact."[100] In our era of natural disasters, climate change, global pandemics, and the ongoing specter of bioterror, we are continually invited to think about humanity in relation to its real, hypothetical, or speculative extinction. Nowhere is this more evident than in the resurgence of the disaster film in popular culture. But while earlier disaster movies may have imagined extinction as having some determinate cause (e.g. nuclear war, alien invasion, mad scientists), in contemporary disaster movies extinction just happens, without determinate cause, and without determinate meaning. In *Independence Day* (1996) the threat of extinction comes from outside in the form of alien invasion, a motif that stretches back through H.G. Wells and beyond. But by the time of *The Day After*

Tomorrow (2004), the implication is that the threat of extinction comes from within, as a result of human mis-treatment of the environment. It is a human-caused disaster, rather than that of war and the external threat, that leads to extinction, a motif that can be found in the Irwin Allen produced films of the 1970s. A further step occurs in *2012* (2009), in which even human causality is absent – the cataclysmic effects portrayed in the film seem to just happen, in scenes that are textbook examples of the sublime, in the Kantian sense of a mixture of horror and wonder. Extinction begins to take on a mystical and apocalyptic tone, with only vague and ancient prophesies as indicators of the possible meaning of extinction.

On the one hand, these examples of "extinction cinema" are dominated by biological themes. What is at issue is the survival of the species, and what is under threat is not just the life of the species, but its very existence. On the other hand, these films also reference, implicitly or explicitly, eschatological themes (the apocalypse, the messianic, the resurrection of the dead). These dual views of biology and theology are often one in the same. For instance, the plague theme is at once a biological motif (concerned with the survival of the species), but also a theological motif (attributing the plague to divine retribution). In such instances we see an excess of life as generative and germinal (the nonhuman life of the plague virus itself) confront another life as scarcity and finitude (the preservation of the species). One type of "life" confronts another type of "life." In this way, the biological motif quickly folds onto a theological motif. And here we find a paradox that is, as we will see, at the heart of the concept of life.

As a scientific concept, extinction is distinguished from its theological and apocalyptic variant by the work of naturalists and zoologists such as Georges Cuvier and the Comte de Buffon. Attempting to discover a scientific framework for studying life that would avoid the religious framework of the

Great Chain of Being, the study of fossils became a key locus for investigating the emergence and disappearance of living beings. Cuvier, in particular, became a proponent of "catastrophism," the theory that the Earth is periodically visited by sudden, cataclysmic events that not only radically alter the Earth's geological composition, but the organisms living on the Earth as well. In the late 18th and early 19th century, Cuvier published a number of archaeological studies that established extinction as a scientific reality, culminating in his multi-volume work, *Recherches sur les Ossemens Fossiles de Quadrupeds.*[101] As Cuvier provocatively notes, behind the revolutions of nations there lies another type of revolution, that of the planet itself: "The ancient history of the globe, the definitive term towards which all research tends, is also in itself one of the most curious objects to have captured the enlightened mind; and, if one allows oneself to follow, in the infancy of our species, the nearly invisible traces of so many extinct nations, one will also find there, gathered in the shadows of the Earth's infancy, the traces of revolutions anterior to the existence of all nations."[102]

Extinction, however, is a strange idea – it simultaneously denotes the negation of particular lives, as well as the negation of an entire category of living beings (the species). Extinction implies death, but death of a particular type – while individual people may die, they do not become extinct, whereas this or that species may be threatened by or in danger of extinction. Extinction also presumes an ontology with respect to the emergence and passing away of life forms. This ontology is predicated on a division between the life of the organism and the life of the species. If, for the individual organism, life is biological life, inscribed within the dichotomy of life and death, growth and decay, and so on, then for the species, life is inscribed within the existence of a category, and the dichotomy of existence and non-existence. If organisms live and die, then species exist or do not exist.

But immediately questions arise: Can one have an organism without a species? Can one have a species without an organism? In a sense, the life of the organism is not the same as the existence of the species (insofar as the death of a single organism does not indicate the extinction of the species), although the concept of the organism presumes a prior concept of species. The category of species presumes the actual possibility of the organism (except in supernatural horror...), however this category may also persist even if there is no actual and living organism to authenticate it. What, then, is extinction? Can it be solely understood as the non-existence of the categorical species, when that non-existence is indelibly tied to the living or dying of actual, living organisms? Or is "extinction" neither simply the organism nor simply the species, but a particular relationship between them?

Such questions are ramified by further one: Who is the witness of extinction? In the case of the extinction of all human beings, who is it that gives testament to this extinction, to the very thought of extinction? In this sense extinction can never be adequately thought, since its very possibility presupposes the absolute negation of all thought. In a short, satirical essay entitled "The End of All Things," Kant notes this paradox: "For we see nothing before us now that could teach us about our fate in a future world except the judgment of our own conscience, i.e. what our present moral state, as far as we are acquainted with it, lets us judge rationally concerning it."[103] Any postulation about the state of the world after the end can only be speculative – and, for Kant, this means that any speculation about the end of all things can only be based on our moral assumptions and prejudices about the world as a human-centric world, a world-for-us. All that remains will be "those principles we have found ruling in ourselves during the course of our life," which will inevitably determine any speculation about the afterlife, "without our having the slightest ground to assume that

they will alter in the future."[104] *Extinction is always speculative.*
Ray Brassier encapsulates Kant on this point, noting "extinction
is real yet not empirical, since it is not of the order of
experience."[10]

But if extinction implies the thought of extinction, and if, in
the case of human extinction, this thought implies the existence
and affirmation of the human, then it would seem that extinction
also has a flip side, in which extinction also implies the non-
existence of all thought (including the thought of extinction),
thereby affirming not the human but the negation of the human,
or the unhuman. In this, even the principle of sufficient reason
slips through our grasp, putting us in the difficult position of not
even being able to assume a reason for the world as such. This
leads Kant to ask, somewhat wryly, "why do human beings
expect an end to the world at all? And if this is conceded to them,
why must it be a terrible end?"[106]

Hence the real question is not whether or not the world will
end, but how this horizon of thought can be thought at all.
Certainly in the history of science, extinction draws upon
zoology, archaeology, and paleontology to gloss this paradox of
the thought of extinction. Here extinction as a biological concept
is different from the death of the organism. But philosophers
such as Heidegger also differentiate this death of the organism
(which for Heidegger is "perishing") from Death, the latter
related to the Being of beings in their temporal being-in-the-
world (*Dasein*). In this sense Death is not just the perishing of the
individual being (while the species still remains intact), but
rather the culmination, condition, and ultimately the negation of
this *Dasein*.

If extinction is tied to the first kind of death (death-as-
perishing), then what is the relation of extinction to this second
kind of death (Death as fulfillment of *Dasein*)? There is a relative
extinction, which entails the death-as-perishing of all existent
living beings that are members of a species, even though in a

scientific sense the species X still remains as a category. But there is also an absolute extinction, which we might describe as relative extinction that binds with it the non-existence of the species X. This is akin to forgotten, unknown, or even imaginary species. From this one can outline an entire "organon of extinction," drawing upon examples from the horror genre. This would involve: the living being without a species (e.g. the unnameable thing); the species without any existent living beings (e.g. cryptids, imaginary creatures); or the subtraction of the species from living beings (e.g. elemental, nonorganic life).

However, if absolute extinction implies that there can be no thought of extinction, then this thought in itself leaves but one avenue open: that extinction can only be thought, that it can only be said to exist, as a *speculative annihilation*. This would be opposed to the idea that extinction describes an event (actual or virtual), or that extinction is the experience (or impossibility of experience) of death-as-perishing on a mass scale, or that extinction is a measurable scientific datum.

Extinction is a void – or, perhaps, a biological void, a form of life that is neither biological life (the death of the organism) nor the existence of a set (the persistence of a species). In extinction, the set is related to life by the way in which the death of life leads to emptiness or the empty set. Extinction is the null set of biology.

Extinction, then, would seem to be more like the non-being of life, understood as the life of a species; it implies the death of individuated living beings, but its primary meaning is that an entire category of life – a set of life – ceases to exist as such. But we double back again, for the concept of the extinct species may still, of course, exist (e.g. in a natural history museum), though the species as such has ceased to exist. Extinction can only imply "life," then, to the extent that a claim is made for the "life" of the species as a whole (e.g. its growth in numbers, its territorial expansion, its speciation or evolutionary adaptation). But the life of the species is still quite different from the life of the individual organism; the latter seems to provide at best an analogy for the former. Extinction is *the non-being of life that is not death.*

8. Life as Non-Being

What is striking about many of the attempts to ontologize life is the way in which "life" becomes an always-receding horizon. If we accept the Aristotelian distinction between Life and the living as structuring the philosophy of life in the West, then it would seem that Life is always receding behind the living. This is the limit of natural philosophy, beyond which one must have recourse to either natural theology or what Kant calls onto-theology, the system of knowledge of the "being-of-all-beings."

But, in the tradition of Aristotelian natural philosophy, Life is not simply the absent center to every instance of the living. The relation between Life and the living is that, while the former conceptually guarantees the latter, in itself it is never available to thought. This, however, does not mean that Life is a concept of negation because it is privative, for its lack of "thisness" is precisely what exceeds any particular instance of the living. If Life has a negative value, then, it is because of its superlative nature, because it exceeds any instance of the living. Any critique of life would have to begin from this presupposition of the superlative nature of Life. Life is "nothing" precisely because it is never some thing, or because it is always more than one thing.

In this sense, philosophical thinking about life borrows heavily from the tradition of mystical theology – and in particular from the tradition of negative theology. Before Anselm offers his famous ontological proof for the existence of God (God as "that beyond which nothing greater can be thought"), the 9th century Irish philosopher John Scottus Eriugena provides one of the most elaborate theories of the divine as "nothing" (*nihil*).

Eriugena's *Periphyseon* (*The Division of Nature*, ca. 866-67) is deeply influenced by the apophatic approach of Dionysius the Areopagite. But the *Periphyseon* applies a dialectical rigor not found in the latter's mystical writing. In Book III, Eriugena puts forth a notion of "divine darkness," in which the divine is *nihil* precisely because of its superlative nature: "For everything that is understood and sensed is nothing else but the apparition of what is not apparent, the manifestation of the hidden, the affirmation of the negated, the comprehension of the incomprehensible..."[107]

To what extent can we say that Life is *nihil* in this sense? Once the ontological difference between "Life" and "the living" is collapsed, life subtracts from itself any possibility of an affirmation. What remains is a kind of negative theology, or better, a negative theo-zoology, whereby life always displays some relation to the negation of life. Hence the after-life is not about the dichotomy between life and death, but about a more fundamental relation – that between Life and Being.

One problem has to do with what happens once the concept of "Life" detaches itself from "the living." This is a problem implicit in the *De Anima*, where the concept of *psukhē* is sometimes a life-principle, and sometimes a stand-in for being itself. In a modern context, process philosophy (Bergson, Whitehead) and process theology (Chardin, Steiner) likewise reach a zone in which "Life" becomes convertible with Being – even if the name of Life is process or becoming or flow.

For many, however, all of this is a false problem. The opening sections of *Being and Time* provide what is perhaps the clearest statement on this point. There Heidegger effectively glosses over the fields of anthropology, psychology, and biology as fields which must presume being in order to begin their inquiries about man, mind, and organism. While each of these fields, according to Heidegger, deals in some way with Life, none of them are capable of posing the question of Life as an ontological question:

> ...in any serious and scientifically minded "philosophy of life" (this expression says about as much as the "botany of plants") there lies an inexplicit tendency toward understanding the being of Da-sein. What strikes us first of all in such a philosophy (and this is its fundamental lack) is that "life" itself as a kind of being does not become a problem ontologically.[108]

This "missing ontological foundation" is itself what grounds these fields. The question *that* Life is, is displaced by the question of *what* Life is – or, more accurately, what the domain of the living is. The anthropological category of man, the psychological category of mind, and a general biology of the organism all presume a Being of Life. Where Heidegger leaves off, however, is at the question of whether Life is a species of Being, or whether the ontology of Life in effect transforms Life into Being. His last words on the topic are at once suggestive and opaque: "Life has its own kind of being, but it is essentially accessible only in Dasein."[109]

One point of entry is to think about non-Life (a non-Life that is not Death), and by extension, non-Being (a non-Being that is not Nothing). Put another way, the challenge would be to think the relation between Life and Being as mediated by negation. This is, to be sure, an ancient problem, one posed by the presocratics, in the attempt to secure a conceptually sound concept of the One and the Many. At its root is the problem – really, the profound ambivalence towards – the concept of non-Being. As Emmanuel Levinas notes, in language not far removed from Eriugena:

> When the forms of things are dissolved in the night, the darkness of the night, which is neither an object nor the

quality of an object, invades like a presence. In the night, where we are given to it, we are not dealing with anything. But this nothing is not that of pure nothingness. There is no longer this or that; there is not "something." But this universal absence is in turn a presence, an absolutely unavoidable presence...There is is an impersonal form, like in it rains, or it is warm.[110]

Thus the problem of non-Being is not simply that of a fear of nothingness or the vacuum. Rather, it is the quite gothic fear of a something whose thingness is under question. "This impersonal, anonymous, yet indistinguishable 'consummation' of being, which murmurs in the depths of nothingness itself we shall designate by the term there is...The rustling of the there is...is horror."[111] The pinnacle of this type of horror – really a kind of concept-horror – is the evisceration of all noological interiority: "horror turns the subjectivity of the subject, his particularity qua entity, inside out."[112]

What is the "there is" of Life? Is the concept of Life already a "there is," and therefore already enveloped in the gothic horror of absolute otherness and anonymity? If "Life," as opposed to "the living," is always receding into the anonymous "there is," does this then mean that Life is really Life-without-Being?

9. Anonymous Horror

Granted, there is a certain absurdity in asking about the non-being of Life; one might as well inquire into non-existent creatures...which is, of course, precisely what the domain of supernatural horror does. Horror film is replete with examples of the horror of the "there is..." The titles of such films are telling: *The Being, The Creature, The Entity, It's Alive!, It Lives Again, Monster Zero, The Stuff, Them!, The Thing*, and so on. Such films imagine the monster in a decidedly different way from the classical creature-feature films (*Dracula, Frankenstein, The Wolf-*

Man, The Mummy). In these films, the site of horror is not simply that of a physically threatening monster, for at least these can be given names (Dracula, Frankenstein's monster, Wolf-Man), and thereby included within the sphere of moral and theological law. This also means they can be destroyed. But what of the creature that cannot be named, or that is named in its unnamability? The unnamable creature is also the unthinkable creature. This would be the B-horror version of Beckett's *L'innomable* (*The Unnameable*). In some cases the unnamable creature is without form, the intrusion of a raging, inverted hylomorphism. Cold War films such as *The Blob* and *Caltiki the Immortal Monster* exist in a state of oozing, abject, borderlessness. In other cases the unnamable creature is without matter, existing as pure (demonic) spirit, an inverted theophany. In *Fiend Without A Face*, human beings are besieged by immaterial, brainstem-like entities, suggesting telepathy as a form of contagion.[113]

These films represent a subtle subversion of the classic creature-feature by shifting the criteria by which a monster is made. Whereas the creature-feature films define the monster as an aberration (and abomination) of nature, the unnamable creature is an aberration of thought. The classical creature-features still retain an element of familiarity, despite the impure mixture of categories (plant, animal, human) or differences in scale (giant reptiles, ants, leeches, etc.). Films featuring unnamable creatures, by contrast, contextualize the monster in terms of ontology (form-without-matter, matter-without-form) or in terms of onto-theology (the spiritual abject, the oozing abstraction). They point towards a form of life-after-life that highlights conceptual aberrations.

Let us pause for a moment and gather together our propositions concerning this concept-horror, or, granting ourselves some poetic license, what we can also refer to as the "teratological noosphere":

The question of an ontology of life is traditionally predicated on a fundamental distinction between Life and the living, or, between that-by-which-the-living-is-living and that-which-is-living.

This distinction is deployed along two axes, one that requires a "principle-of-life" to structure all manifestations of the living, and another axis, in which the living is in turn ordered according to various "boundaries of articulation."

In the context of Scholasticism, the ontology of life continually oscillates between a natural philosophy of creatures and an onto-theology of the divine nature.

The structure of the concept of life is that of negative theology.

Each of these propositions structures the basic way in which "life" as a concept is thought as such. To this we can offer another proposition, which is that, in its traditional formulations, Life is what is denied of Being. Life bears some minimal relation to non-Being. But this can take several forms. The non-Being of Life can be situated either "above" or "below" the scale of the human – on the one hand there is the strata of Thomist "spiritual creatures" or the strata of Aristotelian creaturely life, while on the other hand there is the strata of demonic multitudes or that of subhuman plague and pestilence. This non-anthropomorphic and even misanthropic quality of Life sustains itself with a certain inaccessibility. Even as Life, in conditioning the living, is able to assert its self-evident character, it also puts forth its noumenal qualities. Kant's statements concerning the teleology of the natural world would have to be qualified: it is because Life is noumenal that it is teleological. But this then means that the ends of Life are also anonymous.

Any question of the possibility of an ontology of life would have to consider "life" as a particular intersection between a biology of a non-conceptual life itself and an onto-theology of transcendence, emanence, and immanence. The problem is that the concept of Life has remained tenaciously non-conceptual, even as it continues to function in a conceptual way in scientific fields such as network science, swarm intelligence, and biocomplexity. The issue is not that Life cannot think its own foundation. Rather, the issue is that Life as a concept must always presume a further question concerning Being. The infamous question "What is Life?" appears to always be eclipsed by the question of "What is Being?" And yet the very idea of Life-without-Being would seem to be an absurdity for philosophy…though, as we've seen, not for horror.

"The Subharmonic Murmur of
Black Tentacular Voids"

Prologue

What follows is an extended commentary on a basic question: *can there exist today a mysticism of the unhuman, one that has as its focus the climatological, meterological, and geological world-in-itself, and, moreover, one that does not resort to either religion or science?* But we must be cautious here: this does not mean a mysticism of the Earth or a mysticism of nature, and it does not mean a mysticism of the human subject or "humanity" in general, much less a mysticism of something as grotesque and vague as "life." Still, the suggestion that something vague called mysticism still exists at all may at first seem a ridiculous, even naïve presupposition. Certainly, as a way of thinking and as a set of contemplative practices, mysticism is today no longer as relevant. This is not only due to the dominance of applied scientific thinking in our globalized, convergence cultures, but it is also due to the hegemony of orthodox, religious extremism in dictating the contours of what may or may not legitimately count as mystical experience.

What follows takes place by way of a poetic text and an accompanying commentary. The poetic text is an anonymously authored poem that has been circulating on blogs, forums, and even in a number of scholarly journals.[114] Because the poem was originally circulated in fragments, its total length is not known, and its rather baroque title – "The Subharmonic Murmur of Black Tentacular Voids" – appears nowhere in the body of the poem itself. In addition, it is unclear whether the poem is of contemporary origin, or whether it is a contemporary translation of an older text (though most are of the opinion it is the former). In spite of all these uncertainties, parts of the poem have been said to have – this is the claim, at least – verifiable geomantic symptoms within the metabolism and physiognomy of those who have, under unspecified conditions, recited its lines. Given this rather melodramatic image of, as one blogger put it, "geomantic shifts in the nature of thought," the current rumors surrounding the poem are noteworthy for the way they implicitly investigate the relationship between the climatology, geopolitics, and the unhuman – and it is in this spirit that the following commentary is written.

Stanza I

A landscape of archaeal
And bacterial species
Living under extreme
Environmental conditions

High temperatures
Ionizing radiation
Hydrostatic pressure
Ultraviolet light
Salinity

Low or high levels of pH
Tolerant of heavy metals
Very low levels of water
Very low levels of light

One dark night
Night more viscous than the dawn
Night that has united the living and the nonliving
Transforming the living in the nonliving.

Commentary on Night. Here the language of night and "extreme environmental conditions" opens onto the enigmatic phrase that opens the last stanza, "One dark night." In its geological description and its more poetic evocations (the refrain of "night" in the last stanza), the poem seems to identify itself as part of the darkness mysticism tradition.

But in what way, exactly, should we understand the references to "darkness"? Earlier texts in the mystical tradition may here be of help. One perspective is provided by John of the Cross, the 16th century Spanish Carmelite monk, whose poem *The Dark Night* offers several definitions of the term darkness. The text that we currently have called *The Dark Night* is actually composed of four different, though interrelated, texts: a commentary known as *The Ascent of Mount Carmel*, a diagram made by John detailing the path of mystical perfection, a poem called "The Dark Night," and a commentary on the poem, written by John himself. It is the latter two texts that will concern us here. It is thought that John wrote the poem and commentary of *The Dark Night* around 1583-1585. Its composition is thus well after John's collaborations with Theresa of Avila in reforming monastic institutions, and also after John's imprisonment and torture at the hands of Church authorities.

The Dark Night is a text very different from the more systematic, more rigorous works in speculative mysticism. At its core is the problem of mystical experience – its structure, its meaning, and the possibility (or impossibility) of its communication. It is thought by modern scholars that John broke off his writing on *The Ascent of Mount Carmel* in order to directly deal with the problem of mystical experience in *The Dark Night*.

The Dark Night is also unique in that, in contrast to other mystical texts, it foregrounds the relationship between the divine and the motifs of darkness and negation. However there are variations in the way that John thinks about darkness in the context of mystical experience. In the poem "The Dark Night," the very first stanza lays out these themes: *One dark night / Fired with love's urgent longings / - Ah, the sheer grace! - / I went out unseen, / My house being now all stilled.*

In the commentary John notes the apparent paradox here: "Why, if it is a divine light...does one call it a dark night?" That is, how is it that the union with the divine, the pinnacle of mystical experience, one that is traditionally described in terms of beatific light, how can this experience here be described in terms of its opposite – darkness, stillness, and negation? In response John provides two definitions of darkness: "First, because of the height of divine wisdom, which exceeds the capacity of the soul. Second, because of the soul's baseness and impurity; and on this account the wisdom is painful, afflictive, and also dark for the soul."[115] The second definition follows the standard devaluation of the senses that is a hallmark of the ascetic tradition. More interesting is the first definition, which seems to imply that "divine darkness" is dark because it exceeds our human capacity to adequately render it intelligible. The divine is dark because we have no concept of it.

Given this, if divine darkness is dark because it is in some sense beyond the human, how then are we able to understand even this much? Does not the assertion of the darkness of divinity itself begin to render it intelligible to us? In response to this John provides another, slightly different definition of darkness. As he notes, "this night, which as we say is contemplation, causes two kinds of darkness or purgation in spiritual persons according to the two parts of the soul, the sensory and the spiritual."[116] Here John's emphasis is less on what darkness is and more on how it affects the subject in the midst of mystical experience. This definition is also a much more "philosophical" one, in that it takes the metaphysical split between body and spirit as being affected by divine darkness, but in two different ways. The "sensory darkness" is akin to a privation, again as per the practices of ascetic monasticism. The "spiritual darkness" also appears to be a privation, but more in terms of what John elsewhere calls "spiritual gluttony" (e.g. wanting to be the best

or most extreme mystic for selfish ends; focusing on the desti-
nation and not the journey).

While both of these types of darkness should, obviously, be
read in the context of 16th century Christian mysticism, we can
also draw from them more secular, more philosophical themes.
The sensory darkness is not simply about ascetic discipline; it
also concerns the ambiguous status of empiricism, and the
interface between self and world that ultimately determines all
experience, mystical experience included. Given a radically non-
anthropomorphic concept of God, the question is this: how can
something be experienced, when there is nothing to experience?
In a sense, what John and other mystics call mystical experience
is an oxymoron – and hence the tropes of darkness, night, and
negation.

Similarly, the spiritual darkness John discusses is not simply
about the debasement or demeaning of spiritual practice
(during John's time, when both Inquisitions and Reformations
were afoot, certainly there was no shortage of religious solutions
in the ideological marketplace...). Spiritual darkness extends
the empiricist theme of sensory darkness further. Its primary
concern is with idealism. Given that there is nothing to
experience, what then prevents mysticism from becoming
idealism, a contemplative practice of pure thought, "purged" of
all sensory and phenomenal attributes? John's reply is that the
thought of non-experience is not enough, for then one either
ends up in a vicious circle (the thought of the thought of non-
experience, *ad infinitum*) or one then posits something beyond
thought – at which point thought must itself become silent, still,
and "dark." As John notes, in a sentiment echoed by later
mystical thinkers such as Kierkegaard, "for the intellect faith is
also like a dark night."[117]

In this second definition of darkness – as sensory and
spiritual darkness – John makes a distinction that points to the
limits of both experience and thought. Both types of darkness

are described by John as forms of "purgation" and "accommo-dation" for mystical experience. While the initial part of this process entails active practices (e.g. meditation, contemplation, etc.), the latter part of it is passive. Mysteriously, it just happens. For us, however, living within the non-mystical everyday world, this is not enough. If there is a passive purgation, for what does this cleansing take place? If there is a passive accommodation, what is the subject accommodating?

John's reply comes in the form of his third definition of darkness. It is what we might call the "lightning theory of darkness." As he notes, "in striking the soul with its divine light, it surpasses the natural light and thereby darkens and deprives individuals of all the natural affections and apprehensions they perceive by means of their natural light. It leaves their spiritual and natural faculties not only in darkness but in emptiness too."[118] Here we see the motif of the divine as dark due to its excess and exuberance (as per John's first definition). We also see the notion of the divine as dark because it represents a limit for thought and experience (as per the second definition). Finally, we also have here an articulation of the paradox at the heart of mystical experience: the manifestation of that which is an absolute limit (for experience, for thought, for the human), which, in its manifesting, is also a vacuousness, a dissipation, a receding into shadows and night.

This is the contradictory movement evoked in later thinkers such as Georges Bataille: "Here darkness is not the absence of light (or of sound) but absorption into the outside."[119] Or again, from Bataille's mystical poem "L'Archangélique": "the excess of darkness / is the flash of a star."[120] It is this paradoxical movement that John evokes when he states, "and God is also a dark night to the soul in this life."[121]

Stanza II

Generating models
Of primordial life, and
The opacity of
Non-planetary ground.

The phylogeological distribution
Of other extremophiles
In distant cladograms
Does not provide evidence of their possible antiquity.

Given the shortened gap in descriptions
Of xenobiological transition between
The probiotic synthesis of biochemical compounds
And the last common ancestor (LCA) of all extant living being

Water and ice in the solar system
Giving witness to the extinction
Of ice-dependent organisms
On Earth

Even as the signatures of life – or life itself – are
In evidence, in extraterrestrial ice

Commentary on Ground. In the second stanza of the poem, terms evoking both terrestrial and non-terrestrial environments are more frequent, as are the biological descriptions of "primordial life" and such. All of these terms bring to the mind the concept of the "ground," not only in the literal sense of a planetary, terrestrial land mass, but also in the figurative, philosophical sense of providing a rational basis or support for the development of a concept.

But grounds are often unsteady, shifting suddenly and

giving way to tectonic upheavals that could only have arisen as a result of long-term, nearly imperceptible shifts. For every ground, then, there is a corresponding state of the groundless, or better, an *unground*. The idea of the unground is found in the work of the German mystical philosopher Jakob Böhme. Böhme worked as a cattle herder and a shoemaker before becoming involved in mystical theology, largely as a result of his own mystical experiences (one of which included a vision of the structure of the world encapsulated in a beam of sunlight on a pewter dish). His influences are eclectic, and range from Neoplatonism to Renaissance alchemy. And, while Böhme wrote on a range of topics, from natural philosophy to the theology of the Trinity, it is in mystical works such as the *Von der Gnadenwahl* (*On the Election of Grace*, 1623) that Böhme puts forth the idea of the divine as *Ungrund*.

The term *Ungrund* is difficult to translate, as it may, depending on context, mean a lack of ground, a lack of ground as itself a ground, or a superior or superlative ground. For the sake of simplicity let us translate *Ungrund* as "unground," keeping in mind the plurality of meanings it may have. These pluralities, moreover, are implicit in Böhme's writing. What does it mean to say, as Böhme did, that God is the *Ungrund*? On the one hand God is the unground because the divine is without specific attributes. The divine is "neither light, nor darkness, neither love nor wrath, evil nor good."[122] That is, it is precisely that which is neutral with respect to human-centric, moral and metaphysical attributes of the world. On the other hand, Böhme will repeatedly refer to the divine less in terms of its neutrality, and more in terms of negation – the divine as "the nothing and the all," or simply, the divine as a "Divine Abyss." Here God is Abyss not because the divine passes beyond the human world of morality and metaphysics, but because the divine subtracts itself, in an act of self-negation, from its very intelligibility as such.

This leaves Böhme with a basic theological problem, which is how to explain the creation of the world, nature, and life if the divine is indeed to be negatively thought of as the unground or Abyss. There is, to begin with, the metaphysical problem of how something can be created from nothing. Then there is the theological problem of how plurality, the diversity of the world, can come from an indivisible unity. But beyond these problems, there is another, more important one, which is that if the divine is indeed the unground, and if the unground is neutral, anonymous, and indifferent, then this clearly implies a notion of the divine as equally neutral, anonymous, and indifferent with respect to us as human beings and the human world that we inhabit. The divine as *Ungrund* implies not only negation or a Divine Abyss, but the divine as indifferent to the human.

Here Böhme relies upon a fairly standard mode of theological exegesis for his time, combining the Neoplatonic emanation of the divine with the Trinity as its mode of manifestation, all of which results in the world as manifestation of divine goodness (the *mysterium magnum*), animated by an equally divine and beneficent principle of life (the *spiritus mundi*). In short, Böhme's religious commitment to a highly moralized natural philosophy ends up compromising the ambivalence in his idea of the Divine Abyss or the unground. That the divine as unground eventually leads to the infusion of divine creation in the innately good and moral world is both unsurprising and disappointing.

This is precisely where later philosophers influenced by mystical traditions intervene. A case in point is Schopenhauer's notion of the Will. Schopenhauer's major work, *The World as Will and Representation*, takes up and modifies the Kantian distinction between the world as it appears to us (phenomena) and the world in itself (noumena). For Kant, the latter idea is philosophically necessary but can never be known as such. It is simply there to designate a some thing "out there" that we as human beings sense, study, and produce knowledge about, but which forever remains beyond the pale of human knowledge. In the Kantian framework, the world-in-itself guarantees that all thought does not reduce to idealism.

For all his pessimistic grumblings, Schopenhauer remains optimistic that the world-in-itself can be known by us as human beings. As we noted earlier in this book, Schopenhauer grants to Kant the world as it appears to us, which he terms *Vorstellung*. (Representation). But this is only an index to something else, which, Schopenhauer is sure, is the world-in-itself, which he terms *Wille* (Will). Given that the world-in-itself can never be known without becoming the world as it appears to us, how can Schopenhauer make this claim? Certainly the term "will" here has little or nothing to do with the pedantic world of individual human wants and desires. But what then is it? Nietzsche, one of Schopenhauer's greatest advocates and sharpest critics, notes that Schopenhauer can only make this claim by a "poetic intuition" – by definition it can never be definitively proved.

In attempting to describe the *Wille* as the world-in-itself, Schopenhauer variously resorts to the language of force, flux, flow, process, power, and dynamism, though none of this language is used with any consistency. Neither does Schopenhauer opt for the sort of pantheism evidenced in the *naturphilosophie* of his contemporaries Schelling and Hegel (of whom he has only derisory things to say). Instead, the rhetoric Schopenhauer returns to again and again is that of the ground and the groundless. As he notes in one of his more pessimistic moments, "everything in life proclaims that earthly happiness is destined to be frustrated, or recognized as an illusion. The grounds for this lie deep in the very nature of things."[123] For Schopenhauer, it is the oscillating experiences of suffering and boredom that come to form this paradoxical ground, a ground that relies on the "poetic intuition" of the mystic more than the logical syllogism of the philosopher.

But Schopenhauer offers another, more rigorous notion of ground in discussing the Will as the world-in-itself. Blind, anonymous, and indifferent to our wants and desires, the Will can never, for Schopenhauer, have a stable ground, either in terms of human experience or in terms of human knowledge. For, as he notes, "there will always remain, as an insoluble residuum, a content of the phenomenon which cannot be referred to its form, and which thus cannot be explained from something else in accordance with the principle of sufficient reason."[124] Again: "Everywhere a ground can be given only of phenomena as such, only of individual things, never of the will itself..."[125]

By evoking this phrase "sufficient reason," Schopenhauer insinuates a world-in-itself without the moral-theological framework that still determined Böhme. A long-standing foundation of Western philosophical thought, the principle of sufficient reason states simply that everything that exists has a reason for existing. It is the very bedrock, the very ground of philosophy. In discussing the Will in terms of the principle of sufficient reason, Schopenhauer suggests that the world literally has no reason. "For in everything in nature there is something to which no ground can ever be assigned, for which no explanation is possible, and no further cause is to be sought."[126] This point is not only the limit of philosophy, assuming as it does the principle of sufficient reason; it is also the hinge upon which mystical thought operates. At such a point, all ground can only turn into the unground: "...the principle of the world's existence is expressly a groundless one...which, as *thing-in-itself*, cannot be subject to the principle of sufficient reason or ground."[127]

And this is where the mysticism implicit in Schopenhauer's projects comes to the fore – except that Schopenhauer's reference points are not only those of Christian mysticism, but those of the mystical strand in Hinduism and Buddhism as well.

Whatever Schopenhauer's errors in his understanding of, say, the Buddhist concept of "emptiness" (śūnyatā), what this engagement with mysticism allows him to do is to pose the problem of the unground as a problem of the human. Schopenhauer's challenge is how to think the world-in-itself apart from any human framework, subtracted from any anthropocentric and even anthropomorphic experience.

If, as both Böhme and Schopenhauer suggest, mystical thinking is intimately related to the ground, then we leave the last word to Dōgen, the Japanese monk and founder of the Sōtō School of Zen Buddhism. In or around 1227, Dōgen, returning from his enlightenment on the mountain of T'ien-t'ung, took it upon himself to write a manual for meditation, known as the *Fukan zazen gi*. The opening passages of the manual, which today exists in several versions, depict a master "sitting fixedly" in meditation. However, to a novice monk, the groundedness of the master's sitting appears to stand in contrast with the ungrounded practice of meditation on nothingness. In fact, Dōgen's telling of this tale even seems to suggest that mystical experience is precisely this ground of the unground, the thinking of not thinking: "Once, when the Great Master Hung-tao of Yüeh shan was sitting in meditation, a monk asked him, 'What are you thinking, sitting there so fixedly?' The master answered, 'I'm thinking of not thinking.' The monk asked, 'How do you think of not thinking?' The master answered, 'Nonthinking.'"[128]

Stanza III

Temperature constrains all life,
In the permafrost,
Hibernating for millions of years or
Decomposing for millions of years.

No well-established growth temperatures
In thermotolerant caves
For living optimally
For any of the Bacteria, Archaea, or Fungi.

The amoeba Echinamoeba thermarum grows
Optimally at $T_{opt} > 50°C$ and is
One of the few truly thermophilic eukaryotes
Of terrestrial, nonanthropogenic environments.

Such environments are enriched in elements
Such as arsenic (As), antimony (Sb), and
Mercury (Hg), such that thermotolerant surfaces
Experiencing evaporation also have

Elevated salinity and, therefore
Halophilic inhabitants.

Commentary on Planets. In this, the third stanza, the poem evokes something more than the natural environments of the planet; it also evokes the materials, substances, and "temperatures" of the planet, an entire planetary ambience. There is, from the view of science, the planet itself, which is inclusive of the atmosphere. There is also, from the view of poetry, the atmosphere, which is paradoxically exclusive of the planet. But how can the planet be excluded from the atmosphere, especially when, in common knowledge, the latter derives from the existence of the former?

In an enigmatic text entitled "The Congested Planet," published in 1958, Georges Bataille attempts something unheard of in mystical traditions: to conceive of a non-human mysticism that would also refuse all forms of anthropomorphic personification. Depicting "a planet congested by death and wealth," Bataille evokes an anonymous, impersonal "scream" that "pierces the clouds." In these clouds and on this planet –

planets and clouds that are to be taken literally, and not metaphorically – Bataille notes, with some ambivalence, that "knowledge is the agreement of the organism and the environment from which it emerges."[129] We might even read into this phrase something more specific – it is the accommodation of the environment to the organism that, in the last instance, constitutes knowledge.

That said, Bataille, notes that "the wager of knowledge opens two paths." The first, perhaps unsurprisingly, is the path of instrumental knowledge. Bataille, however, nuances this as both a philosophical and mythical need for a correlation between organism and environment (which is really the accommodation of the latter to the former). In one movement, the organism is this "unconditioned flight" from the possible into "the impossible that surrounds it." Knowledge only arises, however, by virtue of the conversion of the impossible back into the possible, of the unforeseeable into the foreseeable. "Hazardous flight" is converted into "wise calculation."

While the conventional leftist reading of Bataille would see this as a critique of global industrial capitalism, this is only part of the picture. Bataille is not simply on the side of the "hazardous flight," and he is not simply advocating for the liberation of "the impossible." Both the hazardous flight and the wise calculation belong to the human world, and this world, as Bataille notes, is not always the same as "the planet." The differential between them is that of the world-for-us and the world-in-itself: "human knowledge becomes the calculation of possibility when it orders the totality of things for itself..."[130]

This is the second path that the "wager of knowledge" opens up. Bataille can only state it negatively – yes, we have language, and concepts, and tools, and we thereby apply ourselves to the world, in the world. But the world's deep time and tectonic shifts remind us that "it is nothing that exists *in the last place*: everything is in suspense, over the abyss, the ground itself is the illusion of an assurance."[131] Awareness of the fragility of the human, of the ungroundedness of the ground, the disjunction of the planet from the world, the world-in-itself from the world-for-us – all of this evokes for Bataille an experience that would in an earlier epoch be called mystical experience. Nowhere is this more evident, ironically, than in the precision of our knowledge about geology, paleontology, meteorology, and ecology. The more we learn about the planet, the stranger it becomes to us. "The insignificant, provisional nature of the data of even the most certain knowledge is revealed to me in this way."

Whether Bataille actually succeeds in "The Congested Planet" is certainly up for debate – the melodramatic quality of his writing has meant that vast numbers of graduate students have furtively "skipped over" the poetic parts in favor of the more robust "theory." But it is difficult not to read texts like this in light of the ongoing discourse over climate change. This is also the case with Bataille's project *The Accursed Share* (begun in the late 1960s), the first volume of which opens with these striking words: "Beyond our immediate ends, man's activity in fact pursues the useless and infinite fulfillment of the universe."[132]

Bataille is, obviously, not unaware of the natural resource and energy problem that readily exists at the time of his writing *The Accursed Share*. This is, in fact, the backdrop for his approach, which is "to recognize in the economy – in the production and use of wealth – a particular aspect of terrestrial activity regarded as a cosmic phenomenon."[133] As Bataille rhetorically notes, "isn't there a need to study the system of human production and consumption within a much larger framework?"[134]

In as much as *The Accursed Share* is, in Bataille's words, a work of political economy, it is also very much an expanded view of what terms like "economy," "wealth," and "production" may mean. The economy, in its conventional and narrow, human-centric meaning, in the last instance dips down into the bowels of the viscous planet, which itself can only be known on the radically non-human level of deep time. Bataille is asking for more than a simple marriage of economy and ecology, however. In this "cosmic" perspective, economy is also the wealth, production, and expenditure of the non-human planet: "A movement is produced on the surface of the globe that results from the circulation of energy at this point in the universe."[135]

What would this unhuman, planetary economy look like? To begin with, Bataille distinguishes economy in the conventional sense from this other, cosmic economy. The former – a "restricted" economy – is near-sighted in its goals, and has the human (be it in terms of humanity generally or specific interest groups) as its final goal. The latter – a "general" economy – is the view of the deep time of the planet, its tectonic shifts and atmospheric transformations, all of which takes place indifferently to the human-bound interests of the restricted economy. In the former, we not only see rivers, but also dams, bridges, and occasions for sport. In the latter, our language falters, opting for either the poetic (the ebb and flow of life) or the scientific (fluid dynamics, laminar flow).

The failure of Bataille's project was, interestingly, to insinuate that a better appreciation of the general economy could lead to a critique and even transformation of the all-too-human restricted economy, especially when the latter is by definition indifferent to the hopes and desires of the former. The best he could do – which the later chapters of the *Accursed Share* detail – is to simply document the ways in which we as human beings unknowingly participate in the general economy through the ambivalent rituals of festivals, war, and luxurious squandering.

But if Bataille comes up short in *The Accursed Share*, that same theme of the unhuman planet is taken up, in a different guise, in his almost aphoristic, posthumously published text *Theory of*

Religion. Returning to a theme that governs nearly all of his thought, *Theory of Religion* again evokes the problem of mystical experience, and in particular the mysticism of the unhuman. His starting point is our twofold status as situated, living beings: on the one hand we exist *in* the world, viewing the world as a world-for-us as human beings, with particular needs and desires. Our existing in the world in this way is predicated on a basic separation between self and world, which in turn is predicated on a minimal notion of individuation (I am not you, you are not me, get out of my personal space, etc.).

On the other hand, we also exist *as* the world itself, in as much as we are living beings indelibly bound to the world just as much as are the rain, the buildings, or the internet. Our intimate binding to everything gives us the impression of our interconnectedness and of the interconnectedness of all things, human beings being only one type of thing. Bataille uses the terms "discontinuity" and "continuity," respectively, to describe these two impressions. Sometimes we prefer to keep our distance, have some "alone time." At other times we seek not only community or belonging, but a confirmation of this continuity at the basis of the world-in-itself. For Bataille, this everyday experience is the crux of the mystical dilemma: the experience of continuity (existing *as* world) that can only take place on the precondition of a basic discontinuity (existing *in* the world). Or, put another way, our fundamental discontinuity as human beings in the world has, at its greatest or most extreme limit, an overflowing negation that posits, in a contradictory way, the continuity that is also our own, non-human limit. To exist *as* the world, we must cease existing *in* the world.

Bataille refers to this dilemma, with all its negations and contradictions, as *divinity*: "If we now picture men conceiving the world in light of an existence that is continuous…we must also perceive the need for them to attribute to it the virtues of a thing, 'capable of acting, thinking, and speaking' (just as men do). In this reduction to a thing, the world is given both the form of isolated individuality and creative power. But this personally distinct power has at the same time the *divine* character of an impersonal, indistinct, and immanent existence."[136] This sense – of an unhuman, indifferent, planet, can only be expressed in us as a "powerless horror." However, "this horror is ambiguous." Its ambiguity is that which Bataille attempts to get at in his earlier texts, such as "The Congested Planet." It is a dilemma expressed in the contemporary discourse on climate change, between a debate over the world-for-us (e.g. how do we as human beings impact – negatively or positively – the geological status of the planet?), and a largely unspoken, whispered query over the world-in-itself (e.g. to what degree is the planet indifferent to us as human beings, and to what degree are we indifferent to the planet?).

Stanza IV

Many microbes in the deep sea are not
Autochthonous residents,
Descending to the deep as components
Of phytodetrital aggregates.

Such piezophiles (or barophiles) are
Defined by optimal growth rates
Far beyond atmospheric pressure
Where 1 atm = ~0.1 MPa

An ocean time-series study
A long-term, oligotrophic, habitat assessment
Shows the fraction of group Ia Crenarchaea in the total
     picoplankton
Increase with depth to the deepest site.

D. profundis 500-1T, Japan Sea, P_{opt} = 15MPa
Moritella abyssi 2693^T, Mariana Trench, P_{opt} = 30MPa
Psychromonas profunda 2825T, Eastern Tropical Atlantic, P_{opt} =
    25MPa
A life form in dynamic, cosmic equilibrium
With its environment
Is dead.

Life in space can only occur
Temporarily
In a dormant state –

A cold, ice-covered moon
Of some distant planet.

Commentary on Nothing. In this fourth and last stanza the poem noticeably moves beyond the geological and climatological reference points it has evoked in the earlier stanzas. In particular, the concepts of depth and dormancy (the former in the sea, the latter in ice), open onto the questioning of the "autochthonic" origin of life, and in particular, human life. And it is here that the poem most forcefully opens onto the problem of mysticism that we have been elaborating throughout the commentary.

But what kind of mysticism is this, which gives us only scientific description, experimental data, and taxonomic names? We may, in a general sense, think of mysticism as a vague, impressionistic feeling of wonder or awe that may or may not involve drugs, and that may or may not involve nature hikes and generally blissing out. We can also think of mysticism as actually enabled by an overly optimistic, "gee-whiz" scientific instrumentality, in which the Earth is the divinely-sanctioned domain of the human, even and especially in the eleventh hour of climate change. Neither of these is what we mean by mysticism here. Whether it is of the political left or right, whether it is the affectivist-hippie mysticism or the eschatology-of-oil type of mysticism, in both cases mysticism is ostensibly a human-centric and human-oriented experience. Mysticism in these cases is always a union "for us" as human beings.

Something more is gained, however, by considering mysticism in its historical context. Long considered unworthy of serious scholarship, the study of mysticism and mystical writing was largely inaugurated in the 20th century by Evelyn Underhill's book *Mysticism: A Study in the Nature and Development of Man's Spiritual Consciousness* (1911). Underhill elucidates the logic of mystical thinking, paying particular attention to mysticism as a systematic practice, as well as to the psychology of mystical experience. As she notes, "if we may trust the reports of the mystics…they have succeeded where all others have failed, in establishing immediate communication between the spirit of man…and that 'only Reality,' that immaterial and final Being, which some philosophers call the Absolute, and most theologians call God."[137] As Underhill notes, however, how this communication is established varies a great deal, from canonic statements by the Church Fathers, to anecdotes and autobiographies by spiritual laypeople, to fringe heretical insinuations of pantheism.

In the West, the intermittent flowering of mysticism is often explained in terms of a historical context against which mysticism operates. In the 14th century one finds mysticism flourishing in Germany, most notably in the work of Meister Eckhart. While Eckhart remains one of the more "philosophical" mystics, his mode of thinking also works against the hyper-rationality of Scholasticism and its predilection for logic, nominalism, and elaborate Scriptural exegesis. In the 16th century one again finds mysticism flourishing, this time in Spain, where works of, and collaboration between, John of the Cross and Theresa of Avila are the most commonly-cited examples. Tending more to non-philosophical discourses than their predecessors – mystical poems, autobiography, meditations – both authors are working in an ambivalent relation to the emerging scientific humanism of their time. At the core of their writings is the problem of human suffering in the world – indeed, the extent to which suffering *is* the very relation between self and world. As John notes, "the darkness and trials, spiritual and temporal, that fortunate souls ordinarily undergo...are so numerous and profound that human science cannot understand them adequately." John continues, noting that "nor does experience of them equip one to understand them. Those who suffer them will know what this experience is like, but they will find themselves unable to describe it."[138]

Given this, it is no surprise to see many mystics positing some type of effacement or union of self and world as the resolution to the problem of suffering. In effectively bypassing the self-world division one also bypasses all of the corporeal, spiritual, and existential suffering that is part and parcel of that division. This then places one – to the extent there is a "one" any longer – in a position to experience a further effacement or union, that between the earthly and the divine, between the natural and the supernatural. This is the benchmark of nearly every text in the speculative mysticism tradition. But there is often disagreement on exactly how this union of natural and supernatural is to be achieved, let alone described in our all-too-human language. For some, the union is described using the motif of light, a motif that has a long tradition that extends back to the mystical texts of the Church Fathers, and ultimately to Neoplatonic sources (e.g. the divine topologies of light and radiation in Plotinus). This "light mysticism" is also an affirmative mysticism; it asserts a positive communion with God, and it dictates the correct steps on the ladder of this ascent.

But light mysticism is compromised in several respects, including a highly anthropomorphized God with which one enters into a disturbing, paternalistic embrace. If the divine – and here let us say "divine" rather than "God" to emphasize the anti-anthropomorphic tendency – is not simply a super-human but in some radical way beyond the human (or even, against the human), then it follows that any human thought of the divine can only be a horizon for thought. For other mystical thinkers, the very inconceivability of this union with the divine meant that any possible knowledge of it, and any possible description of it, could only take place by a negative means (e.g. the divine is not-X or not-Y, X and Y denoting earthly, human-centric attributes). Hence the preferred motif is not light – be it the radiation of divine Intelligences or beatific light – but instead that of darkness and night. This too has a long tradition, one that extends back to Dionysius the Areopagite, who, sometime in the 6th century, had articulated the *via negativa* or path of negation as the way to divine union. Those in this tradition often utilize several modes of discourse to talk about the divine: that of negative theology, in which one makes use of language, logic, and philosophical argumentation to demonstrate the aporetic unknowability of the divine, and that of darkness mysticism, in which poetry and allegory are used to suggest the ways in which the divine remains forever beyond the pale of human thought and comprehension. John of the Cross's poem "The Dark Night of the Soul" is, along with the anonymous 14th century text *The Cloud of Unknowing*, often referred to as a key text in this darkness mysticism tradition.

Darkness mysticism is not only figuratively but historically the dark underside of mystical thought. Even at the apotheosis of divine communion, darkness mysticism retains the language of shadows and nothingness, as if the positive union with the divine is of less importance than the realization of the absolute limits of the human. Darkness mysticism is "mystical" not because it says yes to the therapeutic, anthropocentric embrace of God, but because it says no to the recuperative habits of human beings to always see the world as a world-for-us.

But, whether one opts for light or dark mysticism, the question that modern scholars such as Underhill return to is this, summarized in Henry Annesley's *Dark Geomancy*: "unless the history of the mystics can touch and light up some part of this normal experience, take its place in the general history of the non-human, contribute something towards our under-standing of non-human nature and destiny, its interest for us can never be more than remote, academic, and unreal."[139] In short, what does mysticism mean to us, in the "ordinary non-mystical"? Underhill's response – a response that has continued to be echoed down to the present day – is that the history of mysticism "is vital for the deeper understanding of the history of humanity."[140]

While Underhill's book is an invaluable study of mysticism, I would suggest that we retain her question, while jettisoning her answer. And here we can, perhaps, see the darkness mysticism tradition in a new light, which is that of our current geopolitical imaginary of climates, tectonic plates, tropical storms, and the viscous geological sedimentation of oil fields and primordial life. In a contemporary context, one in which we are constantly reminded of the planetary (and cosmic) frailty of human beings, and reminded in ways that appear to be utterly indifferent to the "history of humanity" – floods, earthquakes, wildfires, hurricanes, water shortages, extreme temperatures, and the like – in such a context, perhaps something called mysticism has an unexpected meaning. Rudolph Otto suggests this in his exami-nation of the ambivalent "horror of the divine" in religious and mystical experience. Such experiences, in which the human confronts, in a paradoxical state, the absolutely unhuman, can only be thought negatively. In the West, Otto argues, there have been two major modes in which this negative thought has been expressed: silence and darkness. To these Otto adds a third, which he finds dominant in Eastern variants of mystical experience, which he terms "emptiness and empty distances," or the void. Here the negation of thought turns into an affirmation, but a paradoxical affirmation of "nothingness" or "emptiness." As Otto puts it, "'void' is, like darkness and silence, a negation, but a negation that does away with every 'this' and 'here,' in order that the 'wholly other' may become actual."[141]

Hence our opening inquiry – a new darkness mysticism, a mysticism of the unhuman, which is really another way of thinking about a mysticism of the "without-us," or really, a *dark mysticism of the world-in-itself*. This sentiment is expressed in the work of the Kyoto School philosopher Keiji Nishitani, who repeatedly returned to the modern "tendency toward the loss of the human."[142] Nishitani is part of a generation of Japanese philosophers equally versed in Western philosophy and Mahāyāna Buddhism. Nishitani himself studied with Heidegger in the late 1930s, and he frequently engages with Western thinkers such as Schopenhauer, Nietzsche, and Meister Eckhart. For Nishitani, the insight of mystical thinking is to have revealed the core problem of nihilism in the modern era. Echoing Nietzsche's diagnostic, Nishitani notes how modern nihilism is primarily a privative nihilism, in which some thing is revealed to be nothing, in which some locus of meaning or value is revealed to be illusory and empty. For Nietzsche it was the waning of the credulity of religious belief that constituted this nihilism, but for Nishitani it is the twofold waning of religion and science that contribute to the sense of "the nihility that one becomes aware of at the ground of the self and the world."[143] Without a foundation to give meaning and substance to the world, modern nihilism finds itself confronted with nothingness.

Our response, argues Nishitani, should not be to rediscover some new ground for giving meaning to the world, be it in religious or scientific terms, and neither should we be satisfied to wallow in despair at this loss of meaning, this "abyss of nihility." Instead, we should delve deeper into this abyss, this nothingness, which may hold within a way out of the dead end of nihilism. For Nishitani, then, the only way beyond nihilism is through nihilism. And here Nishitani borrows from the Buddhist concept of *śūnyatā*, conventionally translated as "nothingness" or "emptiness." In contrast to the *relative nothingness* of modern nihilism, which is privative, and predicated on the absence of being (that is, an ontology), Nishitani proposes an *absolute nothingness*, which is purely negative and predicated on a paradoxical foundation of non-being (that is, a meontology).

"Emptiness in the sense of *śūnyatā* is emptiness only when it empties itself even of the standpoint that represents it as some 'thing' that is emptiness."[144] How does one think of this strange nothingness beyond nothing, this emptiness beyond the empty? Nishitani frequently turns to planetary, climatological, and cosmic tropes in describing absolute nothingness: "...just as nihility is an abyss for anything that exists, emptiness may be said to be an abyss even for that abyss of nihility. As a valley unfathomably deep may be imagined set within an endless expanse of sky, so it is with nihility and emptiness. But the sky we have in mind here is more than the vault above that spreads out far and wide over the valley below. It is a cosmic sky enveloping the earth and man and the countless regions of stars that move and have their being within it."[145]

In Nishitani's interpretation of absolute nothingness (*śūnyatā*), that through which everything exists and subsists is not itself an existent, nor is it an existent foundation for all existents – it is nothingness, emptiness. From this follows an equally strange and enigmatic identity of all that does exist: "everyone and everything is nameless, unnameable, and unknowable...And this cosmic nihility is the very same nihility that distances us from one another."[146] For Nishitani, it is from this commonality – of nothing and nothingness – that one passes from relative to absolute nothingness: "In contrast to the field of nihility on which the desolate and bottomless abyss distances even the most intimate of persons or things from one another, on the field of emptiness that absolute breach points directly to a most intimate encounter with everything that exists."[147] Self and world come to be regarded not only as groundless, but, in an enigmatic way, as indistinct as well.

This is, of course, the most difficult thought. It doesn't help anyone. There is no being-on-the-side-of the world, much less nature or the weather. If anything, the apparent prevalence of natural disasters and global pandemics indicates that we are not on the side of the world, but that the world is against us. But even this is too anthropocentric a view, as if the world harbored some misanthropic vendetta against humanity. It would be more accurate – and more horrific, in a sense – to say that the world is indifferent to us as human beings. Indeed, the core problematic in the climate change discourse is the extent to which human beings are at issue at all. On the one hand we as human beings are the problem; on the other hand at the planetary level of the Earth's deep time, nothing could be more insignificant than the human.

This is where mysticism again becomes relevant. But the differences between this contemporary mysticism and historical mysticism are all-important. If mysticism historically speaking aims for a total union of the division between self and world, then mysticism today would have to devolve upon the radical disjunction and indifference of self and world. If historical mysticism still had as its aim the subject's experience, and as its highest principle that of God, then mysticism today – after the death of God – would be about the impossibility of experience, it would be about that which in shadows withdraws from any possible experience, and yet still makes its presence felt, through the periodic upheavals of weather, land, and matter. If historical mysticism is, in the last instance, theological, then mysticism today, a mysticism of the unhuman, would have to be, in the last instance, *climatological*. It is a kind of mysticism that can only be expressed in the dust of this planet.

Notes

Portions of this book have previously appeared in the following publications: *Collapse, Hideous Gnosis,* and *Volume Magazine.* My gratitude to those who have provided feedback and encouragement: BW, CM, EM, ELT, JA, MF, NM, MST, MT, RN, TG, TL, and PM.

1. I use this term "non-philosophical" with caution, in that I wouldn't characterize this book as a book of non-philosophy, at least as described in works such as François Laruelle's *Principes de la Non-philosophie.* However, I will be taking up a number of the orientations of non-philosophy, primary among them an inquiry into the decisional structure of philosophy (here presented as "horror").

2. Arthur Schopenhauer, *The World as Will and Representation* I, trans. E.F.J. Payne (New York: Dover, 1969), §71, p. 412.

3. H.P. Lovecraft, "The Call of Cthulhu," in *The Call of Cthulhu and Other Weird Stories,* ed. S.T. Joshi (New York: Penguin, 1999), p. 139. In the early story "Facts Concerning the Late Arthur Jermyn and His Family," Lovecraft expresses this same sentiment as follows: "Life is a hideous thing, and from the background behind what we know of it peer daemoniacal hints of truth which make it sometimes a thousandfold more hideous."

4. Athanasius, *The Life of Antony,* trans. Robert C. Gregg (New York: HarperCollins, 1980), pp. 13-14.

5. *Mark* 5: 9-10, New International Version. Stephanus New Testament version consulted for Koine Greek.

6. Dionysius the Areopagite, *The Divine Names,* trans. Colm Luibheid, in *Pseudo-Dionysius: The Complete Works* (New York: Paulist Press, 1987), IV.19.716D.

7. Dante Alighieri, *Inferno,* trans. Mark Musa (New York:

Penguin, 2003), Canto V: 30-38, 42-47.

8. Johann Weyer, *On Witchcraft: An Abridged Translation of Johann Weyer's De Praestigiis Daemonium*, ed. Benjamin Kohl and H.C. Erik Midelfort, trans. John Shea, (Segundo: Pegasus Press, 1998), Book V, ch. 28, p. 238.

9. Jean Bodin, *De la Démonomanie des Sorciers* (Paris: Jacques du Puys, 1580), Book II, ch. 8, p. 237. The original passage reads "...tous les Demons sont malings, menteurs, imposteurs, ennemis du genre humain." However Bodin continues with the complicated caveat "...et qu'ils n'ont plus de puissance que Dieu leur en permet" ("...and they have no more power than God permits them to have").

10. *The World as Will and Representation* I, §71, p. 409.

11. Ibid., p. 410.

12. Ibid.

13. Ibid.

14. Frances Yates, *The Occult Philosophy in the Elizabethan Age* (London: Routledge, 2001), pp. 53-54.

15. Henry Cornelius Agrippa, *Three Books of Occult Philosophy*, ed. Donald Tyson, trans. James Freake (Woodbury: Llewellyn, 2009), p. 32.

16. Ibid.

17. Johan Huizinga, *Homo Ludens: A Study of the Play Element in Culture* (Boston: Beacon Books, 1971), p. 10.

18. Ibid.

19. Ibid., p. 57.

20. Ibid.

21. Ibid., p. 10.

22. Cited in Walter Kaufmann's introduction to Goethe's *Faust*, trans. Walter Kaufmann (New York: Anchor, 1962), p. 13.

23. Christopher Marlowe, *Doctor Faustus and Other Plays*, ed. David Bevington and Eric Rasmussen (Oxford: Oxford University Press, 2008), A 1.1, 12-15. Citations refer to either the 1604 "A" text or the 1616 "B" text.

24. Ibid., A 1.1, 50.
25. Ibid., 51-54.
26. Ibid., B 1.3, 1-15.
27. Goethe, *Faust*, I 382-85.
28. Ibid., 418-21.
29. Ibid., 438.
30. Ibid., 434; 447-48.
31. Dennis Wheatley, *The Devil Rides Out* (Ware, Hertfortshire: Wordsworth, 2007), pp. 213-14.
32. Ibid., p. 221.
33. Ibid., p. 243.
34. James Blish, *Black Easter, or Faust Aleph-Null* (New York: Avon/Equinox, 1977), p. 28.
35. Ibid., pp. 131-32.
36. Ibid., p. 157.
37. Ibid., p. 163.
38. William Hope Hodgson, *The Casebook of Carnacki – Ghost Finder* (Ware, Hertfortshire: Wordsworth, 2006), p. 45.
39. Ibid., p. 46.
40. Ibid., p. 173.
41. Ibid., p. 180.
42. H.P. Lovecraft, "From Beyond," in *The Dreams in the Witch House and Other Weird Stories*, ed. S.T. Joshi (New York: Penguin, 2005), p. 24.
43. Ibid.
44. Ibid., p. 25.
45. Ibid., p. 27.
46. Ibid., p. 28.
47. Ibid., pp. 26-27.
48. Ibid., p. 29.
49. Junji Ito, *Uzumaki*, volume 1, trans. Yuji Oniki (San Francisco: Viz Media, 2007), p. 20.
50. Letter from Lovecraft to Farnsworth Wright, 5 July 1927, in H.P. Lovecraft, *Selected Letters II, 1925-1929*, ed. August

Derleth and Donald Wandrei (Sauk City: Arkham House, 1968), p. 150.

51. M.P. Shiel, *The Purple Cloud* (Lincoln: Bison Books, 2000), p. 41.

52. Ibid., p. 40.

53. Fred Hoyle, *The Black Cloud* (New York: Signet, 1959), p. 16.

54. Ibid., p. 29.

55. Ibid., p. 105.

56. J.G. Ballard, *The Wind From Nowhere* (Berkeley: Berkeley Medallion, 1966), p. 101.

57. Ibid., p. 127.

58. Ibid., p. 47.

59. Ibid., p. 42.

60. Fritz Leiber, "The Black Gondolier," in *Night Monsters* (New York: Ace, 1969), p. 14.

61. Ibid.

62. Ibid.

63. Ibid., p. 15.

64. Carl Schmitt, *Political Theology: Four Chapters on the Concept of Sovereignty*, trans. George Schwab, (Chicago: University of Chicago Press, 2006), p. 36.

65. Ibid.

66. Ibid., p. 49.

67. Ibid., p. 46.

68. *The World as Will and Representation* II, p. 467.

69. See *Inferno*, Canto XIV, 22-24: "some souls were stretched out flat upon their backs, / others were crouching there all tightly hunched, / some wandered, never stopping, round and round."

70. Ibid., Canto XIV, 51. An alternate edition by Mandelbaum translates "Qual io fui vivo, tal son morto" thus: "That which I was in life, I am in death."

71. Virgil notes as much, chastising Capaneus for continuing this tirade, his very words becoming his own punishment.

72. Upon seeing the bestial figure of Satan, Dante notes "I did not die – I was not living either!" (*Inferno*, Canto XXXIV, 25).

73. To this one might also point to the creatures that inhabit William Hope Hodgson's *The Night Land*, as well as the weird tales by Clark Ashton Smith, Robert E. Howard, and Frank Belknap Long.

74. H.P. Lovecraft, *At the Mountains of Madness*, in *The Dreams in the Witch-House and Other Weird Stories*, ed. S.T. Joshi (New York: Penguin, 2004), p. 271.

75. One could easily imagine a re-casting of Quentin Meillassoux's "arche-fossil" in terms of the findings of the Miskatonic University Expedition. See William Dyer et al., "A Hypothesis Concerning Pre-Archaen Fossil Data Found Along the Ross Ice Shelf," *The New England Journal of Geological Science*, 44.2 (1936): 1-17.

76. *At the Mountains of Madness*, p. 330.

77. Ibid., p. 331.

78. In its simplest form, dialetheism argues that for any proposition *X*, both *X* and *not-X* are true. Dialetheism therefore works against the Law of Non-Contradiction (defined in Aristotle's *Metaphysics*), but, in order to avoid accepting absolute relativism, it must also accept some form of paraconsistent logic. For more see Graham Priest, *In Contradiction* (Martinus: Nijhoff, 1987).

79. See my article "Biological Sovereignty," *Pli: The Warwick Journal of Philosophy* 17 (2006): 1-21.

80. A great deal of humanities scholarship on epidemics focuses on its modern, germ-theory context. Emily Martin's *Flexible Bodies* (Boston: Beacon, 1994), Laura Otis's *Membranes* (Baltimore: Johns Hopkins University Press, 2000), and Ed Cohen's *A Body Worth Defending* (Duke University Press, 2009), provide views from anthropology, literary studies, and cultural theory, respectively. Jacques Derrida has noted the way in which the political concept of

the enemy has, in a post-9/11 era, centered around autoimmune metaphors, in which the threat comes from within. See Giovanna Borradori and Jacques Derrida, "Autoimmunity: Real and Symbolic Suicides – a Dialogue with Jacques Derrida," in *Philosophy in a Time of Terror* (Chicago: University of Chicago Press, 2003). However, there is also much to learn from the pre-modern discourse of plague and pestilence, which often de-emphasizes the ontology of interior-exterior in favor of a theology of life and life-after-life.

81. For a survey, see the collection *Epidemics and Ideas: Essays on the Historical Perception of Pestilence*, ed. Terrence Ranger and Paul Slack (Cambridge: Cambridge University Press, 1992).

82. For instance, William Bullein's mid-16th century plague pamphlet, *A Dialogue Against the Fever Pestilence* is a sustained allegory in which plague is variously represented as greed, selfishness, and the absence of faith.

83. *Exodus* 7:14-12:42, New International Version.

84. *Revelations* 15-16, New International Version.

85. See the chronicle of Gabriele de Mussis, translated and collected in *The Black Death*, ed. Rosemary Horrox (Manchester: Manchester University Press, 1994).

86. The motif of decay has been developed up most recently by Reza Negarestani, who discusses "decay as a building process" in his article "Undercover Softness: An Introduction to the Politics and Architecture of Decay," *Collapse* V (2010), as well as in his chapbook *Culinary Exhumations* (Boston: Miskatonic University Press, forthcoming). Negarestani adopts two approaches to understanding the concept of decay – that of mathematics (derived from Medieval Scholasticism as it developed at Oxford) and that of architecture (particularly the architecture of morphology and transformation). There is much

to expand upon here in the relation between architecture and resurrection. The ruin may be one conceptual link between them.

87. Here is De Mussis' account, which is thought by most historians to be second-hand: "The dying Tartars, stunned and stupefied by the immensity of the disaster brought about by the disease, and realizing that they had no hope of escape, lost interest in the siege. But they ordered corpses to be placed in catapults and lobbed into the city in the hope that the intolerable stench would kill everyone inside...And soon the rotting corpses tainted the air and poisoned the water supply, and the stench was so overwhelming that hardly one in several thousand was in a position to flee the remains of the Tartar army...No one knew, or could discover, a means of defense." In *The Black Death*, p. 17.

88. Homer, *The Odyssey*, trans. Robert Fagles (New York: Penguin), XII.13-15.

89. Ibid., XI.38-42.

90. *1 Corinthians*, 15.38, 42, 44, New International Version.

91. The most sophisticated account of such debates remains Caroline Walker Bynum's study *The Resurrection of the Body in Western Christianity, 200-1336* (New York: Columbia University Press, 1995).

92. Rudolf Otto, *The Idea of the Holy*, trans. John Harvey (London: Oxford University Press, 1958), p. 13.

93. Ibid., p. 28.

94. This is a theme of much literary criticism on the gothic novel. See, for instance, S.L. Varnado's essay "The Idea of the Numinous in Gothic Literature," in *The Gothic Imagination: Essays in Dark Romanticism*, ed. G.R. Thompson (Pullman: Washington State University Press, 1974), pp. 11-21.

95. Kant, in the *Lectures on Philosophical Theology*, notes the following: "God knows all things as they are in themselves

a priori and immediately through an intuitive under-standing. For he is the being of all beings and every possi-bility has its ground in him. If we were to flatter ourselves so much as to claim that we know the *modum noumenon*, then we would have to be in community with God so as to participate immediately in the divine ideas...To expect this in the present life is the business of mystics and theosophists...Fundamentally Spinozism could just as well be called a great fanaticism as a form of atheism" (trans. Allen Wood and Gertrude Clark, Cornell University Press, 1978, p. 86).

96. Aristotle, *De Anima*, trans. Hugh Lawson-Tancred (New York: Penguin, 1986), II.1.412a, p. 157.

97. Aristotle, *De Generatione et Corruptione*, trans. Harold Joachim, in *The Basic Works of Aristotle*, ed. Richard McKeon (New York: Modern Library, 2001), I.5.321a.30, p. 489.

98. Ibid., I.5.321b.36-322a.1-3, p. 490.

99. The different positions of biocomplexity, developmental systems biology, and the various branches of cognitive science today raise these questions.

100. Maurice Blanchot, *The Writing of the Disaster*, trans. Ann Smock (Lincoln: University of Nebraska Press, 1995), p. 1.

101. The full title is *Recherches sur les Ossemens Fossiles de Quadrupèdes, òu l'on Rétablit les Caractères de Plusieurs Espèces d'Animaux que les Révolutions du Globe Paroissent avoir Détruites.*

102. Georges Cuvier, *Recherches sur les Ossemens Fossiles de Quadrupeds* (Paris: Déterville, 1812), "Discours Préliminaire," p. 2.

103. Kant, "The End of All Things" (1794), in *Religion and Rational Theology*, ed. and trans. Allen Wood and George di Giovanni (Cambridge: Cambridge University Press, 2005), p. 224.

104. Ibid.

105. Ray Brassier, *Nihil Unbound: Enlightenment and Extinction* (London: Palgrave, 2007), p. 238.

106. "The End of All Things," p. 224.

107. John Scottus Eriugena, *Periphyseon (De Divsione Naturae)*, *Liber Tertius*, ed. and trans. I.P. Sheldon-Williams with the collaboration of Ludwig Bieler (Dublin Institute for Advanced Studies, 1981), Book III, 633A.

108. Martin Heidegger, *Being and Time*, trans. Joan Stambaugh (Albany: State University of New York Press, 1996), §10, pp. 43-44.

109. Ibid., p. 46.

110. Emmanuel Levinas, "There is: Existence without Existents," in *The Levinas Reader*, trans. Seán Hand (London: Blackwell, 1990), p. 30.

111. Ibid., pp. 30; 32.

112. Ibid., p. 33.

113. In postmodernity this tradition is extended in films such as Mario Bava's *Planet of the Vampires*, David Cronenberg's *Scanners* and Kiyoshi Kurosawa's *Cure*.

114. See, for instance, the special issue of the interdisciplinary *Journal of Literary Psychoplamsics* (volume 4, issue 6), ed. Sonia Haft-Greene, on "The Post-Mystical," which features scholarly articles on the poem and its relevance.

115. John of the Cross, *The Dark Night*, in *Selected Writings*, ed. Kieran Kavanaugh (New York: Paulist Press, 1987), II.5, p. 201.

116. Ibid., I.8, p. 178.

117. John of the Cross, *The Ascent of Mount Carmel*, in *Selected Writings*, I.2, p. 63.

118. *The Dark Night*, II.8, p. 203.

119. Georges Bataille, *Inner Experience*, trans. Leslie-Ann Boldt (Albany: SUNY Press, 1988), p.17, italics removed.

120. Georges Bataille, "L'Archangélique," *Oeuvres Complètes* III (Paris: Gallimard, 1971), p. 78. This translation is from "The

Archangelic," in *Collected Poems*, trans. Mark Spitzer (Chester Springs: Dufour, 1998), p. 65. The key phrase reads "l'excès de ténèbres / est l'éclat de l'étoile."

121. *The Ascent of Mount Carmel*, I.2, p. 63.

122. Jakob Böhme, *On the Election of Grace and Theosophic Questions* (Whitefish: Kessinger Publishing, 1977), I.3. In the *Mysterium Pansophicum* Böhme is more direct: "The Unground is an eternal Nothing (*Der Ungrund ist ein ewig Nichts*)."

123. *The World as Will and Representation* II, p. 573.

124. Ibid., I, p. 124.

125. Ibid., p. 163.

126. Ibid., p. 124.

127. Ibid., II, p. 579.

128. *Dōgen's Manuals of Zen Meditation*, trans. Carl Bielefeldt (Berkeley: University of California Press, 1990) p. 147; I have removed translation brackets for readability.

129. Georges Bataille, "La Planète Encombrée," *Oeuvres Complètes* XII (Paris: Gallimard, 1998), pp. 475-77. The article was originally published in *La Cigüe* no. 1 (1958) and is translated as "The Congested Planet," in *The Unfinished System of Nonknowledge*, ed. Stuart Kendall, trans. Michelle Kendall and Stuart Kendall (Minneapolis: University of Minnesota Press, 2001). The phrase "planète encombrée" may also be rendered as the "cluttered planet."

130. Ibid., p. 222.

131. Ibid.

132. Georges Bataille, *The Accursed Share*, Volume I, trans. Robert Hurley (New York: Zone, 1991), p. 21.

133. Ibid., p. 20. Allan Stoekl examines this theme in his book *Bataille's Peak: Energy, Religion, and Postsustainability* (Minneapolis: University of Minnesota Press, 2008).

134. Ibid.

135. Ibid., pp. 20-21.

136. Georges Bataille, *Theory of Religion*, trans. Robert Hurley (New York: Zone, 1992), p. 33, translation modified.

137. Evelyn Underhill, *Mysticism: A Study in the Nature and Development of Man's Spiritual Consciousness* (Cleveland: Meridian, 1963), p. 4.

138. *The Ascent of Mount Carmel*, p. 57.

139. Henry Annesley, *Dark Geomancy: Mysticism and Politics in the Age of the Old Ones* (Boston: Miskatonic University Press, 2009), p. 4.

140. *Mysticism*, p. 444.

141. *The Idea of the Holy*, p. 70.

142. Keiji Nishitani, *Religion and Nothingness*, trans. Jan Van Bragt (Berkeley: University of California Press, 1983), p. 89.

143. Ibid., p. 95.

144. Ibid., p. 96.

145. Ibid., p. 98.

146. Ibid., p. 101.

147. Ibid., p. 102.

CULTURE, SOCIETY & POLITICS

Contemporary culture has eliminated the concept and public figure of the intellectual. A cretinous anti-intellectualism presides, cheer-led by hacks in the pay of multinational corporations who reassure their bored readers that there is no need to rouse themselves from their stupor. Zer0 Books knows that another kind of discourse - intellectual without being academic, popular without being populist - is not only possible: it is already flourishing. Zer0 is convinced that in the unthinking, blandly consensual culture in which we live, critical and engaged theoretical reflection is more important than ever before.

If you have enjoyed this book, why not tell other readers by posting a review on your preferred book site. Recent bestsellers from Zero Books are:

Kill All Normies

Online culture wars from 4chan and Tumblr to Trump
and the alt-right
Angela Nagle

"This short head-butt of a book taught me more about recent political events in a single rich evening of reading than I've learned in this entire last and very unpleasant year of obsessively monitoring cable TV..."
George Saunders, 2017 Man Booker Prize Winner
Paperback: 978-1-78535-543-1
ebook: 978-1-78535-544-8

How to Dismantle the NHS in 10 Easy Steps
Youssef El-Gingihy
The story of how your NHS was sold off to private healthcare
and why you will have to buy insurance soon.
Paperback: 978-1-78535-045-0
ebook: 978-1-78535-046-7

Capitalist Realism
Is there no alternative?
Mark Fisher
An analysis of the ways in which capitalism has presented itself
as the only realistic political-economic system.
Paperback: 978-1-84694-317-1 ebook: 978-1-78099-734-6

Rebel Rebel
Chris O'Leary
David Bowie: every single song. Everything you want to know,
everything you didn't know.
Paperback: 978-1-78099-244-0 ebook: 978-1-78099-713-1

Cartographies of the Absolute
Alberto Toscano, Jeff Kinkle
An aesthetics of the economy for the twenty-first century.
Paperback: 978-1-78099-275-4 ebook: 978-1-78279-973-3

Malign Velocities
Accelerationism and Capitalism
Benjamin Noys
Long listed for the Bread and Roses Prize 2015, *Malign Velocities*
argues against the need for speed, tracking acceleration as the
symptom of the on-going crises of capitalism.
Paperback: 978-1-78279-300-7 ebook: 978-1-78279-299-4

Meat Market
Female flesh under Capitalism
Laurie Penny
A feminist dissection of women's bodies as the fleshy fulcrum
of capitalist cannibalism, whereby women are both consumers
and consumed.
Paperback: 978-1-84694-521-2 ebook: 978-1-84694-782-7

Poor but Sexy
Culture Clashes in Europe East and West
Agata Pyzik
How the East stayed East and the West stayed West.
Paperback: 978-1-78099-394-2 ebook: 978-1-78099-395-9

Romeo and Juliet in Palestine
Teaching Under Occupation
Tom Sperlinger
Life in the West Bank, the nature of pedagogy and the role of a
university under occupation.
Paperback: 978-1-78279-637-4 ebook: 978-1-78279-636-7

Sweetening the Pill
or How we Got Hooked on Hormonal Birth Control
Holly Grigg-Spall
Has contraception liberated or oppressed women? *Sweetening
the Pill* breaks the silence on the dark side of hormonal
contraception.
Paperback: 978-1-78099-607-3 ebook: 978-1-78099-608-0

Why Are We The Good Guys?
Reclaiming your Mind from the Delusions of Propaganda
David Cromwell
A provocative challenge to the standard ideology that Western
power is a benevolent force in the world.
Paperback: 978-1-78099-365-2 ebook: 978-1-78099-366-9

Readers of ebooks can buy or view any of these bestsellers by
clicking on the live link in the title. Most titles are published
in paperback and as an ebook. Paperbacks are available in
traditional bookshops. Both print and ebook formats are
available online.

Find more titles and sign up to our readers' newsletter at
http://www.johnhuntpublishing.com/culture-and-politics
Follow us on Facebook at
https://www.facebook.com/ZeroBooks
and Twitter at https://twitter.com/Zer0Books